AMERICAN INDIAN
COOKLORE

AMERICAN INDIAN
COOKLORE

AUTHENTICATED AMERICAN INDIAN RECIPES
SYLVESTER AND ALICE TINKER

OKLAHOMA INDIAN COOK BOOK
MAE ABBOTT

NAVAHO FOODS AND COOKING METHODS
FLORA L. BAILEY

COACHWHIP PUBLICATIONS
Greenville, Ohio

American Indian Cooklore
© 2015 Coachwhip Publications

Authenticated American Indian Recipes, by Sylvester and Alice Tinker
Published 1955

Oklahoma Indian Cook Book, by Mae Wadley Abbott
Published 1956

"Navaho Foods and Cooking Methods," by Flora L. Bailey
Published in *American Anthropologist*, Vol. 42, 1940.

No claims made on public domain material.

ISBN 1-61646-280-9
ISBN-13 978-1-61646-280-2

Cover: Cooks by Acee Blue Eagle

CoachwhipBooks.com

This compilation of early recipe collections brings together two published booklets and one academic paper with recipes from traditional and recent American Indian kitchens. These include submissions from Choctaw, Chickasaw, Osage, Navaho, Sioux, and other cooks.

AUTHENTICATED AMERICAN INDIAN RECIPES
7

OKLAHOMA INDIAN COOK BOOK
57

NAVAHO FOODS AND COOKING METHODS
89

Recipes

AUTHENTICATED
AMERICAN INDIAN
RECIPES

THIS BOOK DEDICATED
IN MEMORY OF

FRED LOOKOUT

PRINCIPAL CHIEF
Of The
OSAGE TRIBE OF INDIANS
1955

PUBLISHED BY SAM McCLAIN
P. O. BOX 2
PAWHUSKA, OKLAHOMA

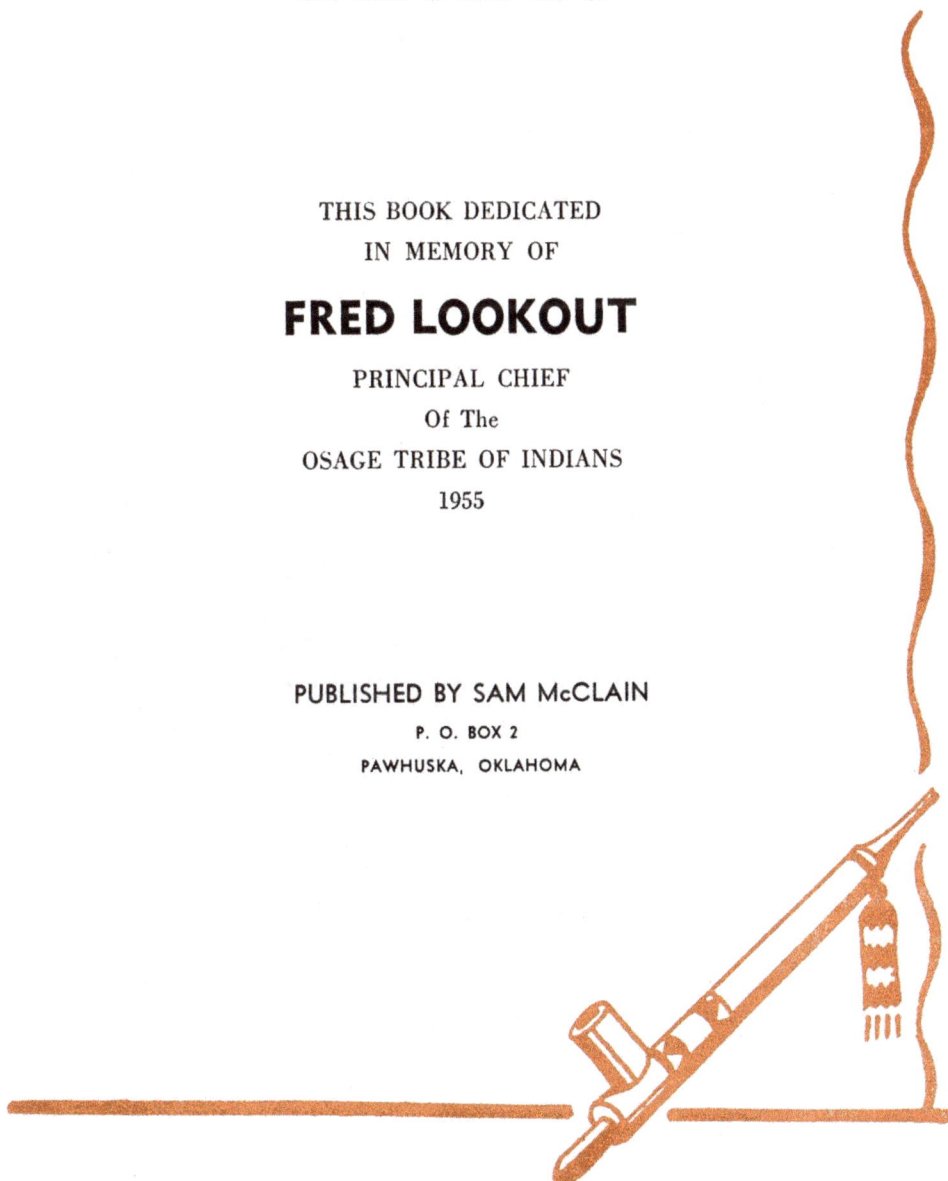

FRED LOOKOUT

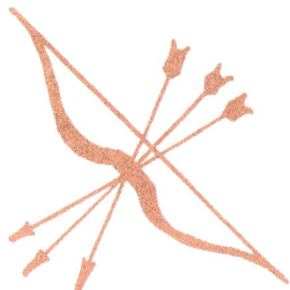

EARLY CUSTOMS AND HABITS OF
AMERICAN INDIANS

HOW THEY EARNED THEIR DAILY BREAD

You have perhaps been told that the Indian woman, who was called a squaw, was the slave of her husband. This is not true. She had her work and he had his. It was his business to chase the game, sometimes many miles, and often it happened when game was scarce that he might be away for days or even weeks. He fought the bears and other wild beasts and sometimes was dangerously hurt. He made weapons and had to be ready at all times to use them.

The women did the work about the tepee, or wigwam, and cultivated the ground and made the clothes. In short, the man did the work belonging to war and hunting, while the women had to do with peace. When the clan or tribe was moving, the women carried most of the baggage, but the man had to be on guard, for an enemy hidden behind a tree might at any time send an arrow toward them.

The Indian seldom spoke crossly to his wife and children, and when they were safe from enemies and there was plenty of food he played games with them.

The young men were very fond of games. The game of lacrosse, which you may have seen played, was an Indian game which our college boys have borrowed.

The Indian baby was called a papoose. He had no crib like the one you used, but his mother was too busy to hold him in her arms, he might be strapped on a board and hung in a tree or against a post. When the mother was traveling she hung him on her back. When he grew larger he helped his mother gather sticks for the fire, or gather berries. He had a little bow and arrow and learned to shoot. He was taught to swim, to run and to climb. He learned to track rabbits and to set traps for them and other small animals. When he grew larger he was taken on hunting trips, and last to war. The first years of the little Indian girls were spent in much the same way. But instead of learning how to shoot she learned to prepare skins for moccasins and for clothing, and to sew skins for wigwams. She also learned how to cook and to cultivate the ground, and in some tribes the women wove coarse cloth, and made baskets and pottery.

The reason the Indians were so often at war was be-

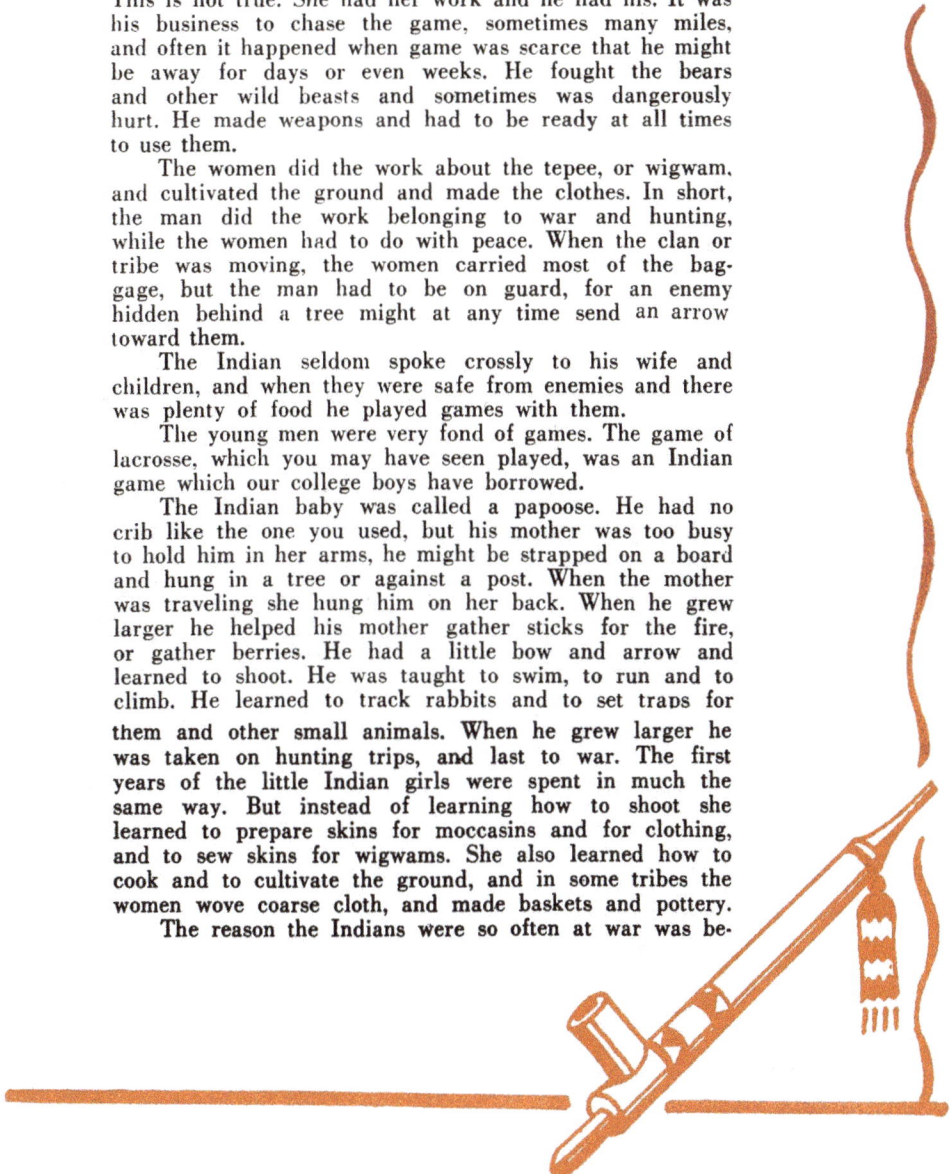

cause of the fact that one tribe hunted on the ground that was claimed by another. Now, people who live chiefly by hunting must have a large territory, for game does not stay in one place like cows and sheep. Sometimes the hunter would go for days without finding anything, or if he did find it, a bow and arrow is not so good a weapon as a gun, and the deer and buffalo got away. So, in order to get close to it, he had to learn to move quietly and to learn to follow tracks. That is why he had keener sight than the white man.

The Indians got most of their food by hunting and fishing but they got some of it from the soil. They had learned how to kill the trees by cutting off a ring of bark around the trunks, or else they burned them down. They scratched the ground among the dead trees or stumps with a stone hoe, or with a stick sharpened in the fire. Then they planted corn and pumpkins, or squash, or sometimes beans, sunflowers, and tobacco. Of course the crop was small with such poor tools, as the ground could not be broken up so that the roots could get food from the soil. The Indians had learned that they could get larger crops if they put a dead fish or two in the hole where they planted the corn.

The corn and sunflower seed were pounded between two stones. Sometimes they found a hard stone **which already had a hole worn part of the way through it by water, and used it to hold the corn while the women pounded with a smaller stone. They mixed the coarse meal with water and baked the cake in the ashes.**

When they were making a journey they parched the corn and pounded it up. In this way they could have something to eat without lighting a fire. The smoke of a fire might have shown their enemies where they were and have been a cause for great danger.

They made pots of clay, but as they could not make them strong enough to stand the fire, they often cooked their food by heating stones and then putting them into the water. Sometimes they dug a hole in the ground and lined it with smooth stones. Then they built a fire in the hole until the stones were very hot. The ashes and coals were then cleaned out and shell fish, green corn and game were put into the hole and covered with grass or seaweed. On the seashore perhaps you have helped in a clam bake.

Some times they cooked meat by hanging it before a fire until it was done, or by broiling it on the coals. Things cooked in this way are so good that one would almost like to turn Indian.

SQUAW BREAD

●

2 tbsps. Baking Powder

1 qt. luke warm water

1 tsp. salt

1 tbsp. compound

Flour enough to make about like biscuit dough. Roll and cut any shape desired. Fry in kettle of boiling compound.

COSTUE (SQUAW BREAD)

●

1 pt. sour milk

1 tbs. Shortening

½ tsp. soda

3 heaping tsps. Baking Powder

1 tsp. salt

Flour enough to make dough easily handled. Knead smooth, roll out to ½ inch thickness. Divide in portions equal to a medium sized biscuit, cut two or three slits in this and cook in a kettle of deep fat as doughnuts.

This should make a piece about the size of a saucer.

SYRUP FOR SQUAW BREAD

●

1 qt. white corn syrup

1 lb. brown sugar

Boil together, use no water

1 tbsp. mapeline

Take from fire and beat into above ½ cup bacon fryings.

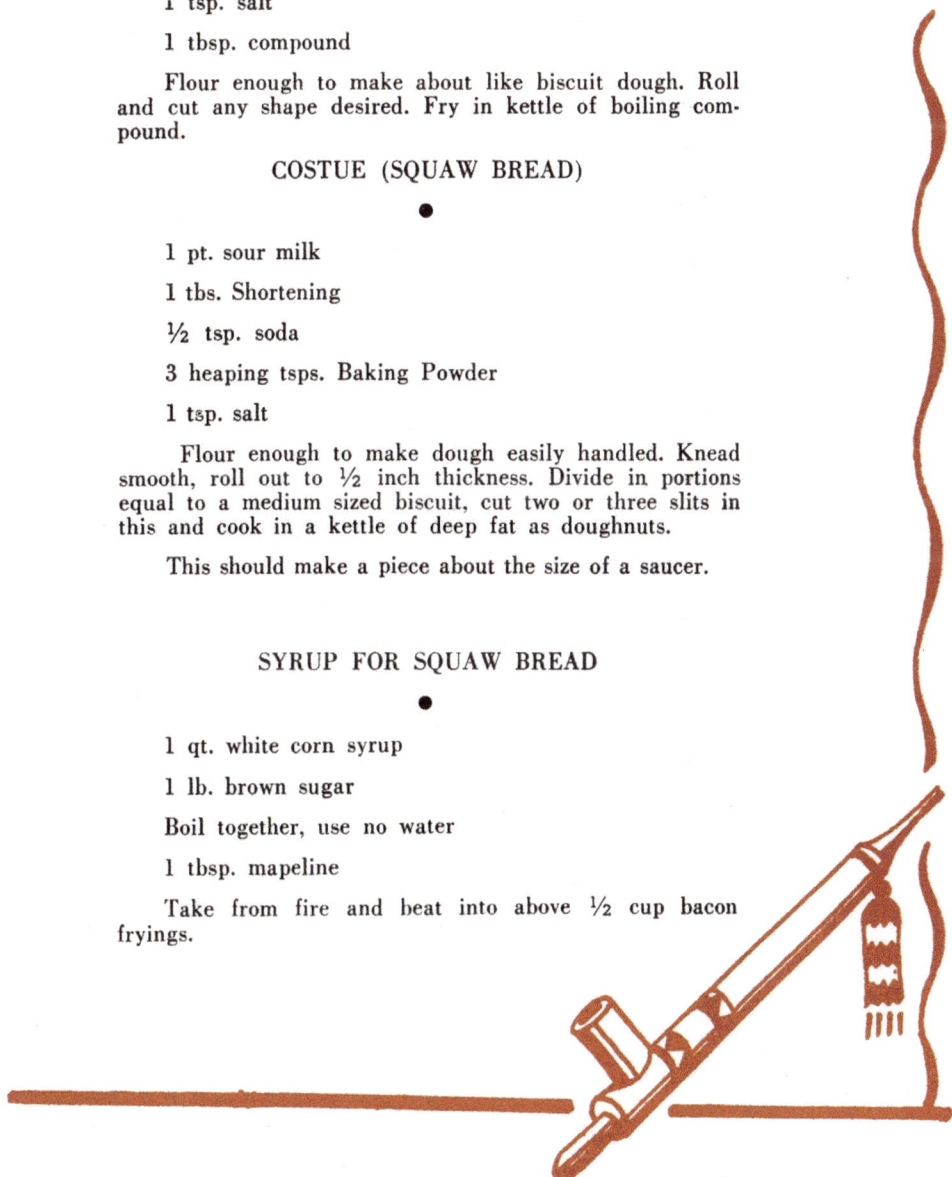

CORN BREAD

●

1 cup sour milk	1 cup white corn meal
1 egg	1 tsp. salt
1 tbsp. melted fat	½ tsp. soda

Mix dry ingredients, then add liquids, hot fat last. Pour into well greased pan, also hot, and bake in hot oven.

INDIAN CORN BREAD

●

6 ears of green corn (roasting ears)

1 tsp. salt

4 tbsps. bacon fryings

Grate the corn from cob, using coarse grater. Add salt and half of bacon grease, mix well. Pour into pan, greased with remaining fryings and bake for 25 minutes in hot oven.

SAUSAGE CORN BREAD

●

4 cups corn meal

2 tsps. salt

½ cup flour

4 tsps. baking powder

Enough warm water or milk to make a thick batter. If using sour milk, add 1 teaspoon soda.

Mix all ingredients together and pour one-half mixture in greased bread pan. Take 1½ lbs. well-seasoned pork sausage and pat out in large thin layer to fit on corn meal mixture. Place remaining corn meal mixture on **top** of sausage and bake in moderate oven until **brown**.

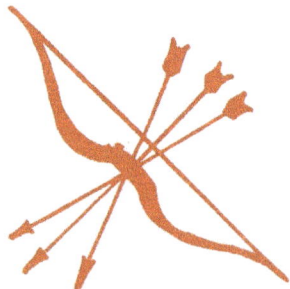

SCRAPPLE

•

Scrapple is a delicious breakfast dish. Take the head, heart, and any lean scraps of pork, and boil until the flesh slips easily from the bones. Remove the fat, gristle and bones, then chop fine. Set the liquid in which the meat was boiled aside until cold, take the cake of fat from the surface and return to the fire. Let it boil again, then thicken with corn meal as you would in making ordinary corn meal mush, by letting it slip through the fingers slowly to prevent lumps. Cook an hour, stirring constantly at first, afterwards putting back on the range in a position to boil gently. When thick enough to mould, pour into a long, square pan, not too deep. When cold cut into slices and fry until golden brown, as you do mush. Roll in seasoned flour.

I cut the scrapple into large squares and store in the deep freeze but it will keep in the refrigerator for several weeks.

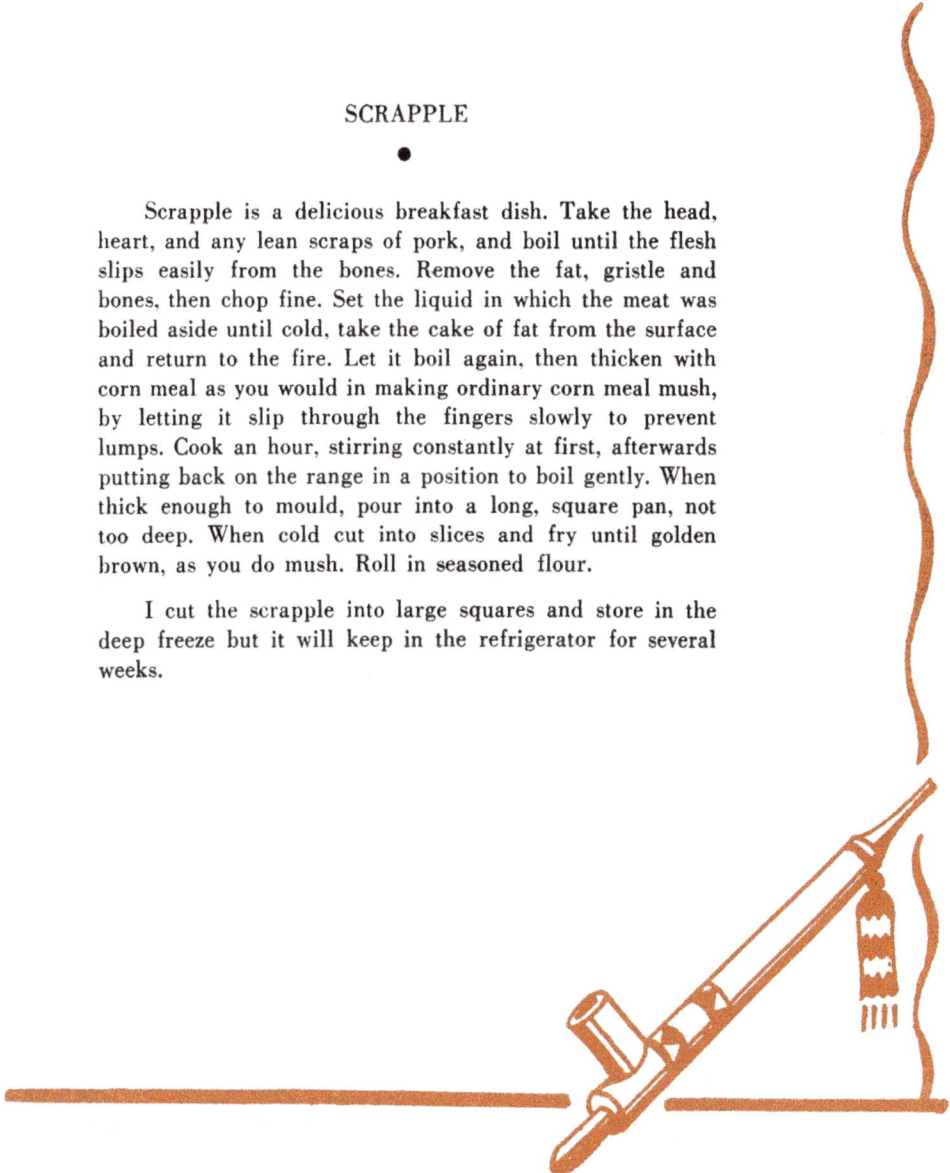

DRIED CORN

3 doz. roasting ears

Shuck and silk corn. Place in large kettle, cover with water and bring to boil; boil for 10 minutes.

Take corn from kettle and cut from cob, being careful to cut kernels out whole. A good way is to take or cut out one row of kernels and then push and cut out remaining corn.

Place corn on canvas covered table out of house in sun and let dry for several days, taking in before sundown and being careful that the corn does not get wet. Store corn in clean muslin bags and let hang on porch to keep cool and dry.

Cook with pork as you do beans.

INDIAN HOMINY

Take 1 gallon of squaw corn (shelled)

Make lye with ashes or take prepared lye and make strong lye solution in enamel kettle. Place corn in lye solution, water being over corn. Bring to boil and let boil for about 15 minutes or until skin slips on corn.

Pour off lye water and place corn in tub full of fresh, cold water until corn feels clean and is not slick.

Place on table on canvas or clean muslin and let dry in sun for several days.

Store in clean flower sacks.

Cook with fresh pork as you do beans.

BAKED WINTER SQUASH

1 medium sized squash

1/4 tsp. salt

2 tbsp. sugar

3 tbsp. molasses

1 1/2 tsp. hot water

3 tbsp. butter

Do not peel but wash squash. Remove seeds, cut in squares, cook in boiling salted water several minutes.

Place squash cut side up in baking dish, sprinkle with salt and sugar. Combine molasses and hot water, pour over squash and dot with butter. Bake in moderate oven 350 degrees 55 minutes or until tender, serves 4.

TO DRY SQUASH OR PUMPKIN

Build a large fire, let flames die down completely to hot ashes and coals.

Take large Hubbard squash or pumpkin, place in hot coals, turning often so as not to burn. Keep turning until squash is well-roasted and has cracked in several places. Take from fire, cut in half and then in 1-inch rings, peel outer skin and also scrape and peel inside.

Take 1-inch thick rings of pumpkin and hang them on poles or place on table in the sun and dry. Take in at night and be careful to keep indoors if it rains.

Store as you would dried fruit. It takes several days to thoroughly dry.

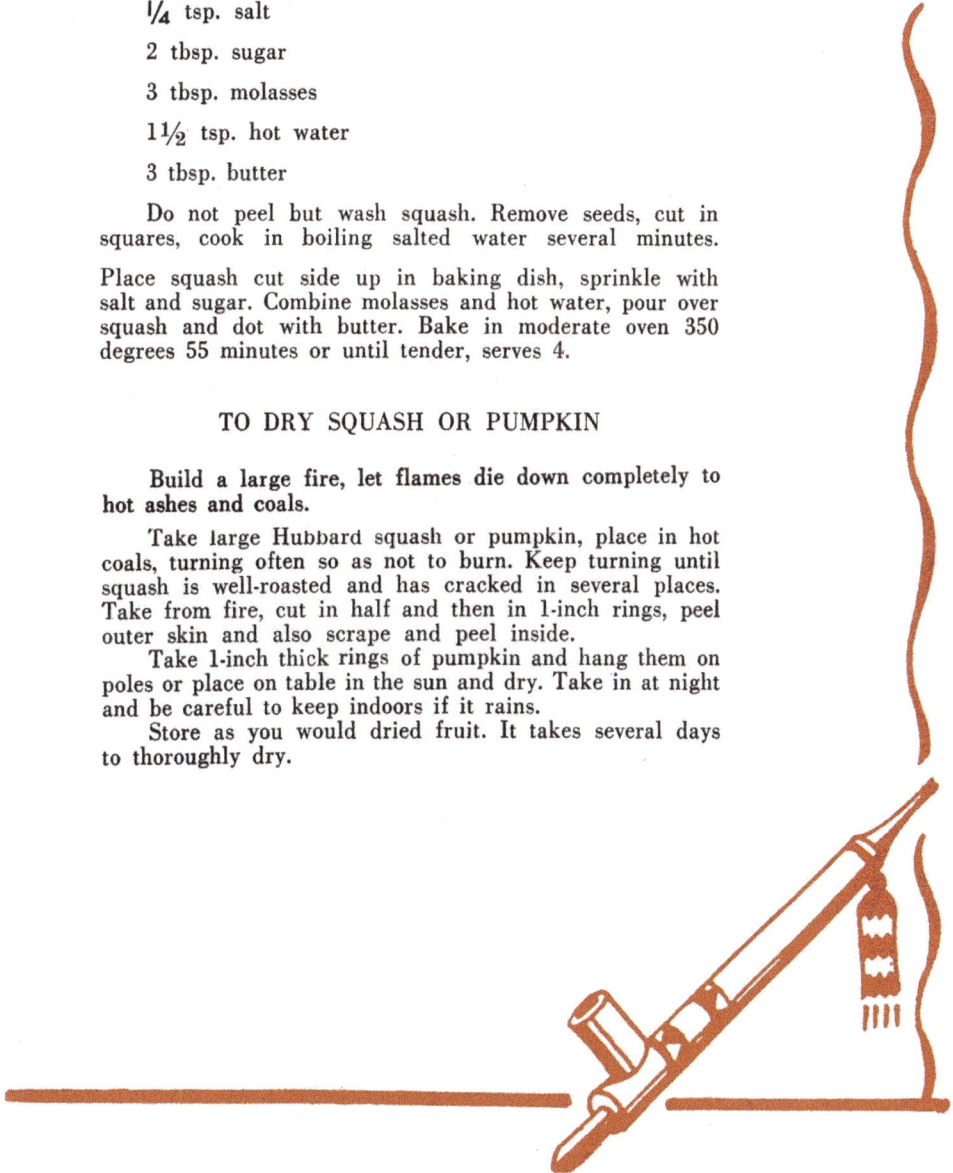

CHEROKEE BEAN DUMPLINGS

1 can kidney beans (well drained)

6 cups corn meal, preferably pounded corn meal

Tallow or suet

Scald meal a little at a time with boiling water until moist enough to mold with hands.

Place kidney beans in corn mixture. Mold this mixture into balls about size of small oranges and place small piece of suet or tallow in center of each ball. Flatten ball with palm of hand and drop into kettle of hot water or meat broth and cook for about 45 minutes or until firm. Delicious with fresh side pork.

INDIAN MUSH

3 cups squaw corn (parched)

Grind or pound in mortar

Sift corn, taking or separating powder from large particles of corn.

Take 1 qt. chicken or meat broth and cook large particles of corn until tender (about 1 hour).

When done mix powdered part of corn in small amount of cold water and add to broth to thicken.

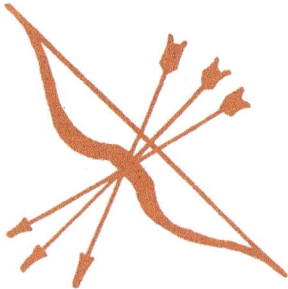

WILD ONIONS AND SCRAMBLED EGGS

Wild onions with scrambled eggs is a delicacy among all Indian tribes. At the first breath of Spring when the green grass has just started to peep through the ground, the lowly onion comes into its glory. For this is the time that the Indian takes to the hidden glades, along little streams, and among sheltered groves. This is the time to hunt wild onions.

Most every family has a secret spot that they keep for their private supply of wild onions. You must dig them with a shovel or spade as the root or onion part is deep in the ground, and the tender root of the onion is to be preferred in place of the top.

The wild onions should be gathered when the tops are from 5 to 6 inches out of the ground. They are very tender at this time. Allow plenty of time for cleaning as it is a tedious task. After they have been cleaned and washed, I keep the onions in a neat bunch. As they are easy to cut if they are in uniform bunches. Chop each bunch very fine, using the tops also. Put 1 cup shortening or bacon fryings in a heavy skillet that has a cover that fits tightly. Heat the fat and add cut onions. Brown lightly until onions are about half done or just turning brown. Add 1 cup hot water and place lid on tightly.

Reduce heat and let simmer until all of liquid has cooked out, stirring frequently to keep from burning. After the water has completely cooked away, add six to eight eggs and scramble together. Salt and pepper to taste. Stir the eggs and onions just until the eggs are cooked. Serve at once.

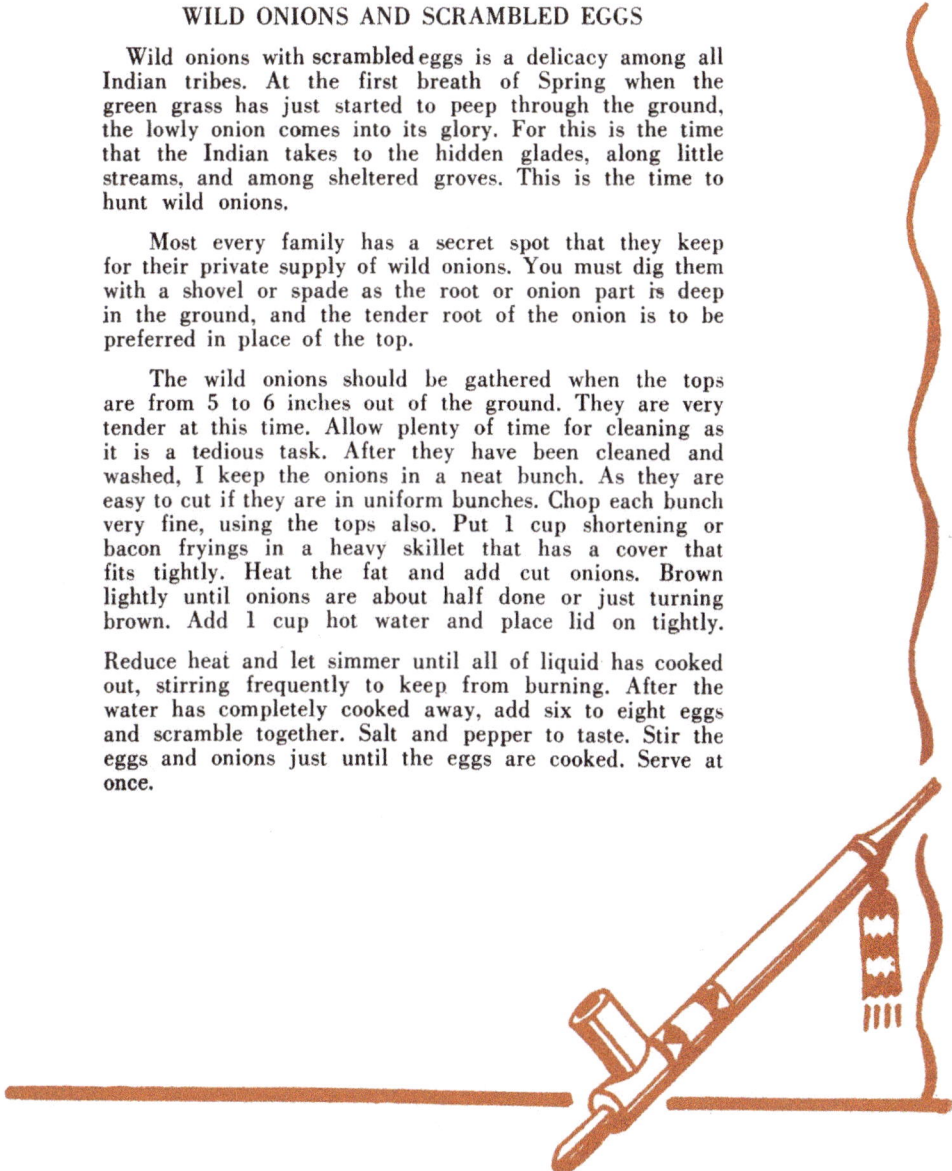

DRIED CORN COOKED WITH DRIED PUMPKIN OR SQUASH

2 cups dried squaw corn

1 lb. fresh pork shank

Place in medium sized kettle as corn will expand.

Cook for two or three hours as you would dry beans. About 45 minutes before corn is done put in several pieces of dried pumpkin or squash. Continue cooking until squash is tender.

YONKA - PINS

(WATER LILY ROOTS)

The Yonka-pin is the root of the water lily and is gathered by the Indians late in the Autumn.

Gather the lily roots by digging deep into the mud and getting the tender roots.

Wherever you see water lilies growing on lakes and ponds, you can mark these places and in the late summer or autumn you can gather these roots.

Scrape the roots clean as you would carrots. Cut into one-half inch pieces. Either cook fresh or string on a stout cord and hang to dry, if kept any length of time.

COOKING METHOD

1 qt. Yonka-pins cut into $\frac{1}{2}$ inch pieces, 1 lb. fresh

pork, salt and pepper to taste. Cook slowly in water to cover, until tender.

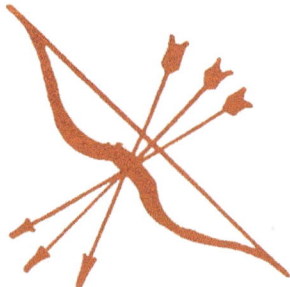

WILD GRAPE DUMPLINGS

●

1 qt. grape juice (Wild Grapes if Available)

1 qt. wild grapes (canned with juice)

1/4 cup sugar

Heat to boiling and add:

2 cups flour

4 Teaspoon baking powder

1/2 teaspoon salt

1 Tablespoon sugar

3/4 cup milk

1/4 to 1/3 cup butter

Mix dry ingredients, sift twice. Work in butter with pastry mixer, fork or finger tips, and add milk gradually. Roll out on floured board and cut in strips, then in squares, drop in hot grape juice or grapes and juice, cover and steam until tender.

HOT GRAPE JUICE

●

1 quart Wild Grape juice or bottled grape juice.

1 Tablespoon flour or corn starch added to 1/4 cup of

the cold juice — mixed to thin paste; add to the remainder of the juice — sweeten to taste and cook over low fire stirring frequently. Delicious as a hot drink. Four or five whole cloves add to the flavor.

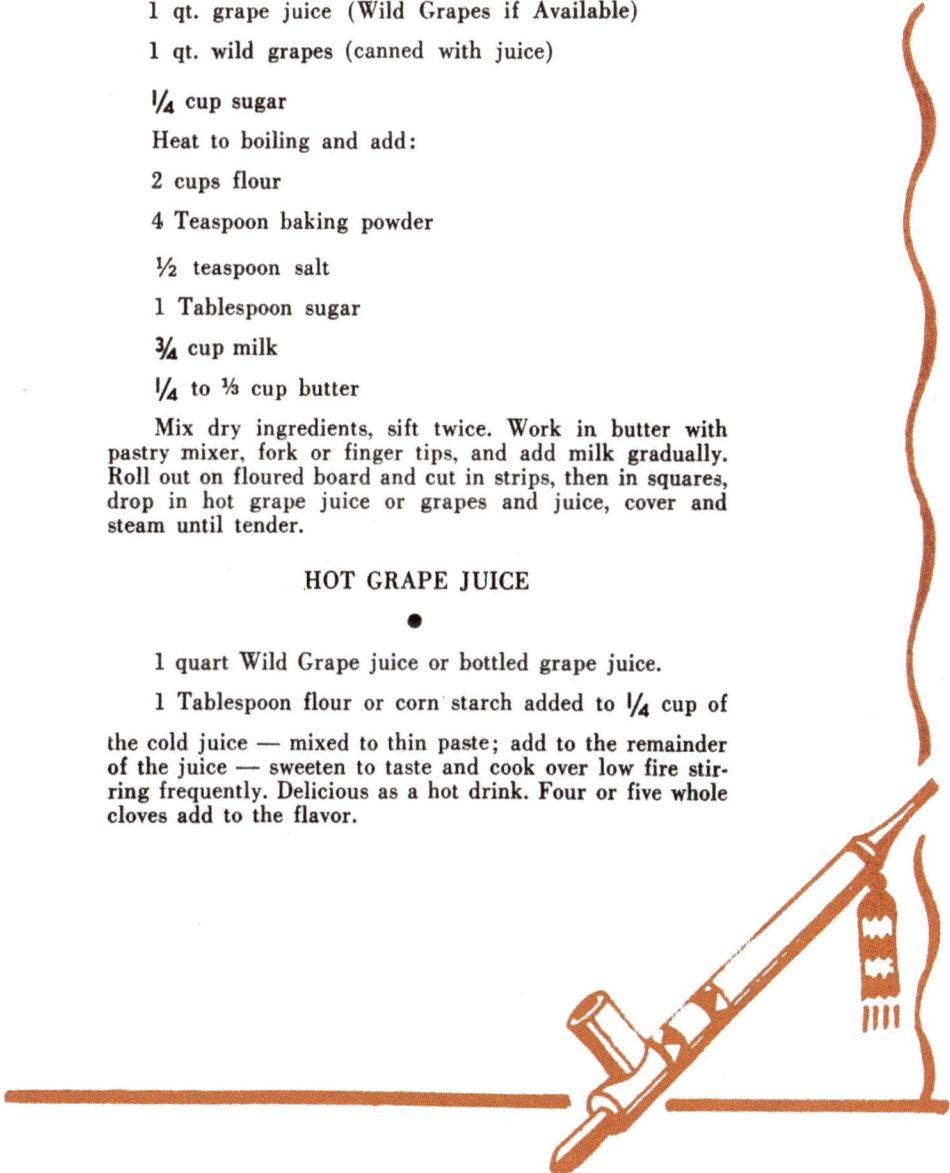

BAKED HUCKLEBERRY
OR BLUEBERRY DUMPLINGS

Roll rich biscuit dough thin, cut it into little squares four inches wide and seven inches long. Spread over with the berries that have been washed and drained and sweetened to taste.

Roll up the crust and put the rolls in a baking pan just a little apart: put a piece of butter on each roll, spices if you like. Sprinkle over one-half cup of sugar, a little hot water. Bake in a moderate oven until brown; serve with whipped cream or sauce made from blueberries.

MOLASSES CANDY — OLD FASHIONED TAFFY

One quart sorghum molasses, one cup brown sugar, four tablespoons butter.

Place all ingredients in a six-quart kettle. Let it boil over a slow fire until it begins to look thick, stirring it often to prevent burning. Cook to hard crack stage or test by dropping a few drops in a cup of cold water. If it hardens quickly and breaks in long threads is has cooked enough. Now put in one half teaspoon of baking soda and stir it well; then pour it out into well buttered flat tins. When partly cooled, take up the candy with your hands, well buttered, then pull and double until the candy is a whitish yellow.

If flavoring is desired, drop the flavoring on the top as it begins to cool, and when it is pulled, it will all be flavored.

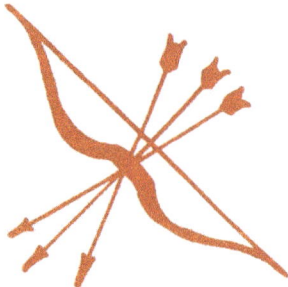

INDIAN CHUTNEY

2 qts. apples

1 lb. raisins

3 c. brown sugar

5 c. vinegar

1 tsp. cayenne pepper

2 qts. green tomatoes

1 small onion

1/2 c. salt

1 oz. ginger

Chop tomatoes, onions and apples, add raisins. Let stand in jar overnight. In morning mix with vinegar and spices. Cook tender and seal.

YELLOW PEAR TOMATO PRESERVES

3 lbs. yellow tomatoes
3 lbs. sugar

6 lemons sliced and seeded

4 oz. preserved ginger or 1 piece ginger root

Method:

Scald tomatoes and slip off skins. Place tomatoes in crock or enameled bowl. Add sugar and allow to stand over-night. Drain juice from tomatoes, add sliced lemons from which seeds have been removed, rind left on, cook until syrup is thick, add tomatoes and ginger, and cook slowly until tomatoes are transparent. If ginger root is used remove from preserves before pouring in to clean hot jars. Seal the jars at once.

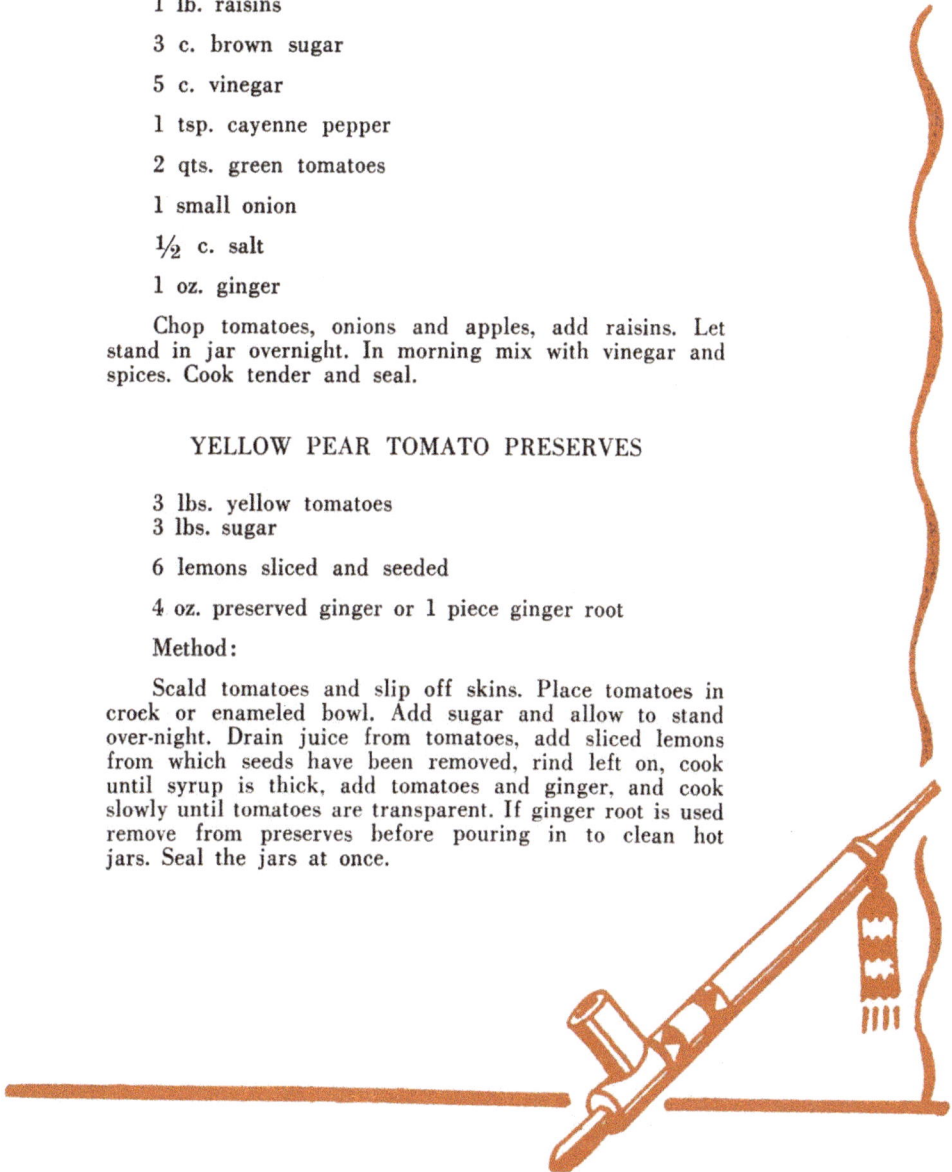

INDIAN CANDY

1 qt. dry squaw corn "parched"

1 cup pecan or hickory nut meats, chopped fine

White syrup to moisten

Grind corn or pound in wooden mortar until fine. Take parched corn meal and moisten with syrup (preferably Karo) until it is moist enough to mold. Now take 1 cup pecan or hickory nut meats and cut fine.

Add nut meats to moist corn and roll into balls, place on wax paper and leave for about 1 hour.

SURPRISE LEMON CAKE

Make favorite pastry. Roll out crust and line pan.

5 tbsp. flour

1 cup sugar

2 egg yolks

1 cup sweet milk

2 egg whites, (beaten separately)

2 tbsp. melted butter

pinch of salt

Grated rind and juice of one lemon

Beat egg yolks, sugar, flour and salt for three minutes or until creamy. Add milk, melted butter, lemon rind and juice. Last fold in egg whites that have been beaten separately. Bake in raw crust for 40 minutes at 350 degrees.

BAKED INDIAN PUDDING

2 tbsp. melted butter	½ cup corn meal (yellow)
½ tsp. cinnamon	4 cups scalded milk
½ tsp. salt	⅓ cup molasses
½ cup seedless raisins	2 eggs
light cream whipped	¼ cup sugar

Gradually add corn meal to hot milk, cook, stirring constantly, until slightly thickened. Add molasses. Beat eggs, add sugar, butter, cinnamon and salt. Add hot milk mixture. Mix well, add raisins. Pour into 1½ quart greased pudding dish. Bake in slow oven, 300 degrees F. for 2 hours. Serve hot with whipped cream. Especially good with vanilla ice cream. Serves 6.

"ENA" (Mothers) PLUM PUDDING

1½ cup finely chopped suet	1 lb. seedless raisins
1 tsp. allspice	1 lb. currants
1 tsp. nutmeg	½ c. nutmeats (cut fine)
1 tsp. cinnamon	2½ c. sifted all purpose flour
2 tsp. salt	2 tsp. baking soda
4 eggs	1 tsp. cloves
1 cup sugar	2 cups molasses
½ cup grape juice	2 cup buttermilk
2½ cups fine dry bread crumbs	

Method for making pudding. Scald raisins and currants, drain thoroughly, combine with nut meats. Dredge with 1 cup flour. Sift remaining flour, baking soda, cloves, all spice, nutmeg, cinnamon and salt.

Beat eggs, add sugar, molasses, buttermilk, suet, grape juice and crumbs. Add raisin mixture and mix well. Next add spice and flour mixture and mix well. Pour into 2 greased 3 lb. molds, cover, steam 3 hours. Cool pudding wrap in heavy waxed paper and store. The pudding keeps for weeks in a cool place. Re-steam to heat, Serve hot with sauce. Each pudding serves 12.

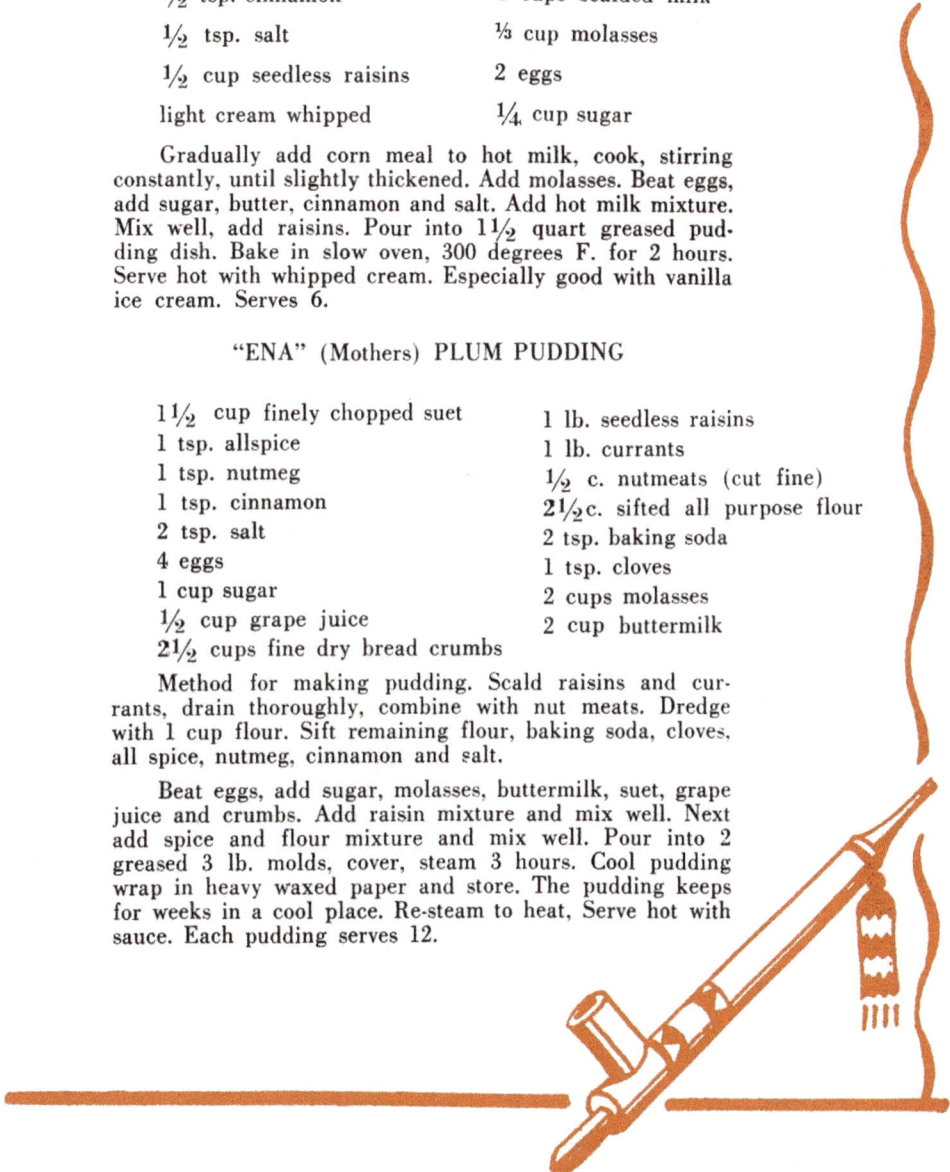

GINGER BREAD

½ cup shortening

½ cup sugar

1 egg

2½ cups sifted all purpose flour

1 tsp. baking soda

1 tsp. cinnamon

1 tsp. ginger

½ tsp. cloves

½ tsp. salt

1 cup molasses

1 cup boiling water

Cream together shortening and sugar. Add egg, beat well. Sift together flour, baking soda, cinnamon, ginger, cloves and salt. Combine molasses and water. Add alternately with flour mixture to creamed mixture. Line 8 x 8 x 2in. greased pan with greased wax paper. Pour in batter. Bake in moderate oven 350 degrees F. for 50 or 60 minutes. Cool five minutes, remove from pan. Slice bananas over top of ginger bread and spread with apricot glaze.

APRICOT GLAZE

Strain contents of a no. 2 can of apricots into sauce pan and add ½ cup sugar, juice of ½ lemon and the grated rind of 1 lemon, bring to boiling point over medium heat. Thicken with 2 tsp. cornstarch dissolved in 4 tbsp. of apricot juice. Cook until thick and clear. Slice bananas on top of ginger bread. Cover with cool glaze. Top each serving with whipped cream.

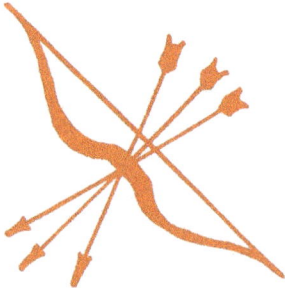

OLD FASHIONED PUDDING SAUCE

1 tbsp. butter

1 tbsp. flour

1 cup boiling water

1 egg

¾ cup sugar

few grains of salt

1 tsp. vanilla or lemon

Melt butter, blend in flour and gradually add hot water. Cook stirring constantly until mixture thickens.

Beat egg, add sugar and salt. Add to cooked mixture. Cook stirring constantly until thoroughly heated. Add extract. Serve hot. Variation: Cook ¼ cup raisins in sauce, add ¼ cup brandy. After removing from fire. This sauce is delicious on mince pie.

CORN MEAL GRIDDLE CAKES

1 cup yellow corn meal

3 tsp. baking powder

1 egg

2 tbsp. molasses

1 cup sifted all purpose flour

¾ tsp. salt

1½ cups milk

¼ cup melted butter

Sift together corn meal, flour, baking powder and salt. Beat egg, add milk. Combine with dry ingredients. Add molasses and butter, mixing smooth. Drop by spoonfuls on hot griddle, spreading thin. Bake, turning to brown on both sides. Serves 4.

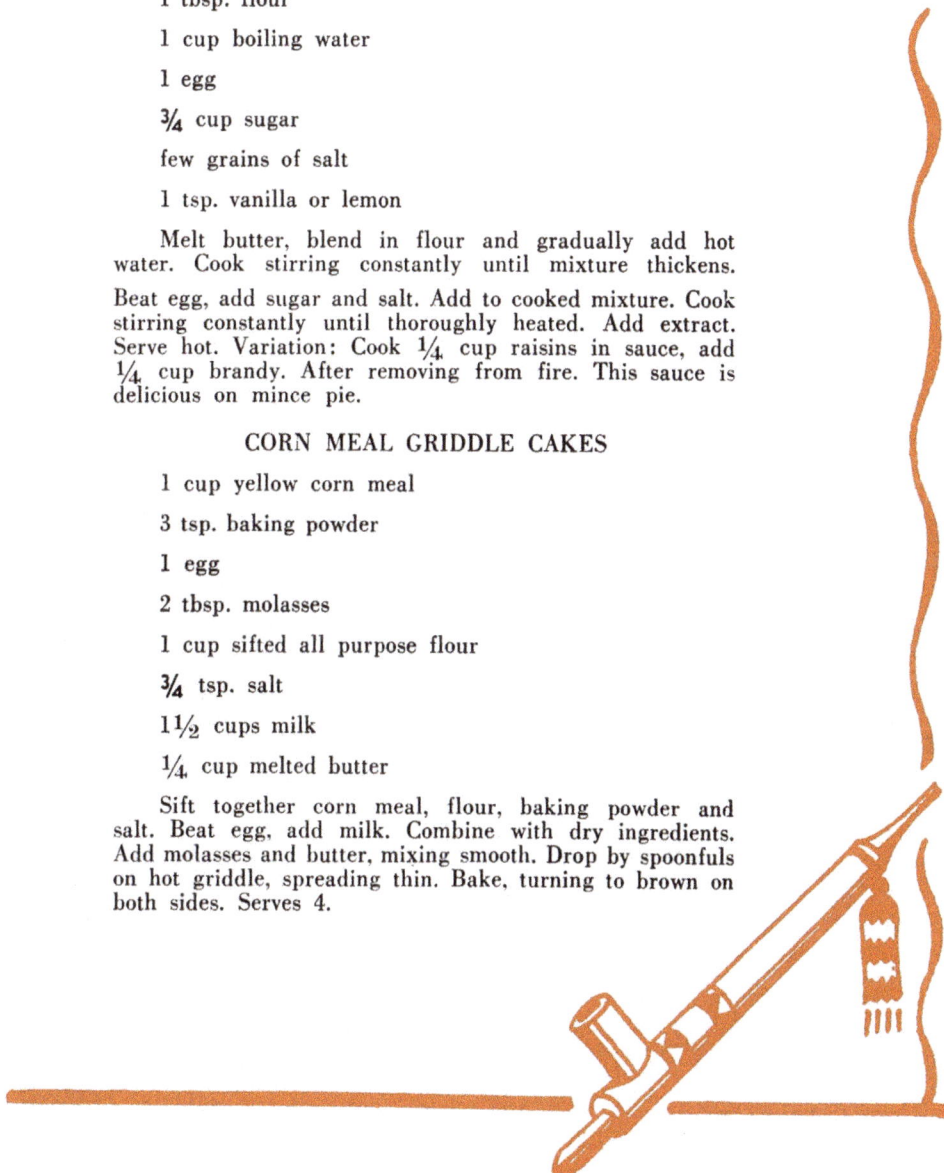

FRIED MEAT PIES

1½ lbs. of round steak, ground coarse with little suet
—salt and pepper to taste.

Make batter of:

2 cups flour

3 tsp. baking powder

1 tsp. salt

Enough sweet milk or warm water to make thick batter,
"very thick."

Make out meat balls about size of large walnut, drop
in batter and see that they are well coated then place
them in kettle of hot fat as for doughnuts.

BAKED MEAT PIE

1½ lbs. of round steak ground coarse with a little
suet. Salt and pepper to taste. Add about 2 tablespoons water.

Mix biscuit dough of—

2 cups flour

1 tsp. salt

2 tsp. baking powder

1 tbs. shortening (level)

1 cup milk

Roll out in small rounds, place meat mixture on one
half, then fold over and crimp edges together—place in
well greased bread pan and bake in moderate oven until
brown.

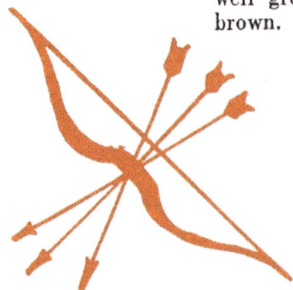

FRANKIE McCLAIN
OSAGE DANCING COSTUME

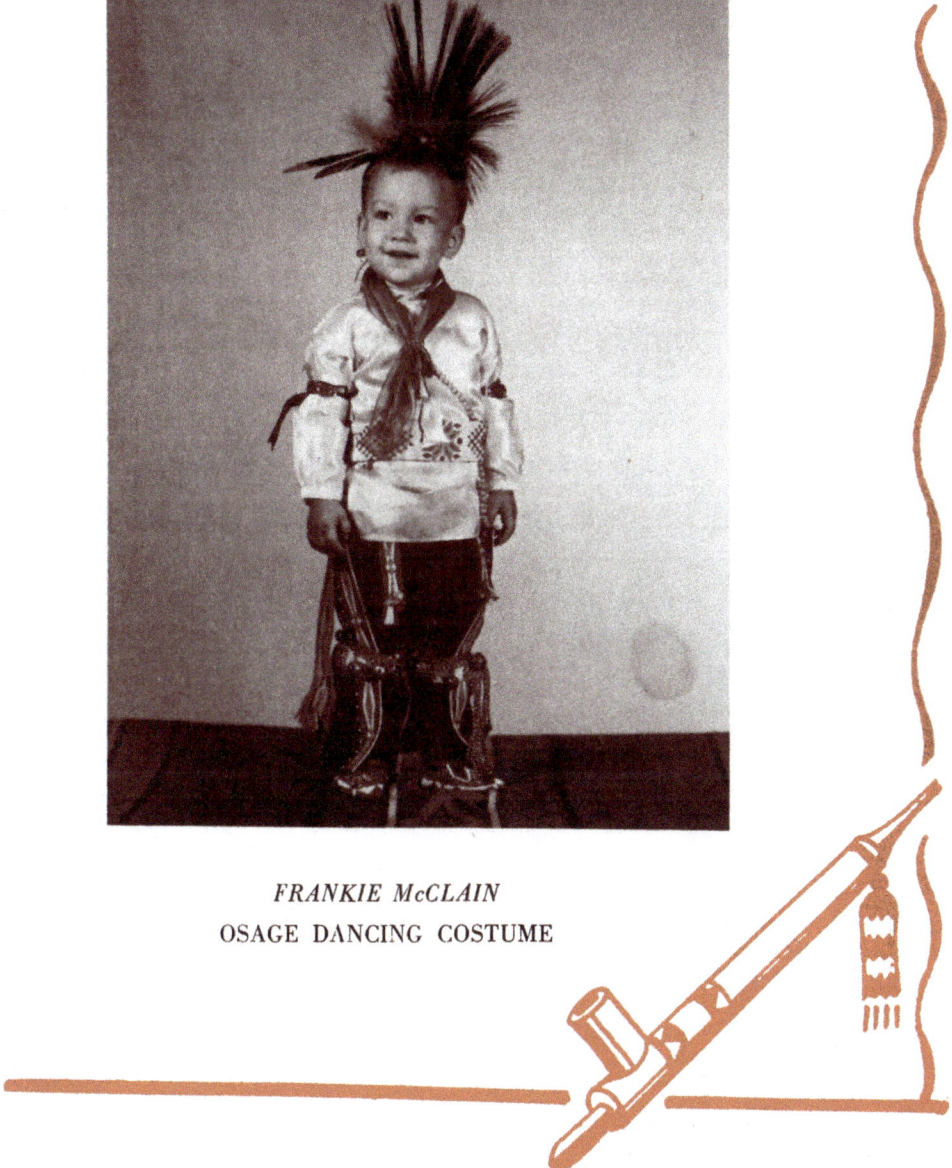

My name is Frankie McClain. My father and mother call me shunka or Chi-bonne', which means boy, in the Indian language.

I am dressed up in my Indian ceremonial dancing costume. My grandmother is going to use this picture for her new Indian recipe book.

I like to dance, and when my grandfather goes to the Indian camp, to dance, I beg to go along, so I can dance when the Indian men beat the big drum.

Another reason I like to go, is because the Indian women are cooking such nice smelling things to eat, over the camp fires. If I look hungry, they give me pieces of barbequed meat and large pieces of squaw bread, hot from the fire.

Sometimes when my grandmother (E-co), is cooking over a camp fire, she lets me cook.

Here are some of the recipes that boys and girls can cook over a camp fire.

After the fire has died down to a good bed of hot coals, go into the woods and cut a long stick from a tree. Use your pocket knife and make a fork on the end of the stick,

The stick must be green or it will burn.

Take the weiners or "Hot-dogs" and put them on the stick, and roast them on a slow fire for ten minutes. In cooking weiners, it is very important to have a little fire, and that burned down well.

If you like something different, split the weiners lengthwise, but not clear through, and insert a strip of cheese. Then wrap a strip of bacon around the weiner securing both ends with a toothpick. Cook on a very slow fire for ten minutes. Have buns and mustard ready for a very juicy sandwich.

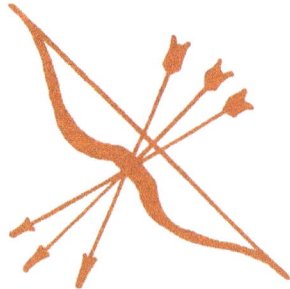

HIDE THE WEINER

1 long medium potato

1 weiner

salt and pepper

$\frac{1}{2}$ tsp. mustard

Peel the potato and use apple corer to make hole. Rub inside of hole with salt, pepper, and mustard. Place weiner in hole. Rub potato with bacon fryings or butter.

Place on aluminum foil, using enough to make a double thickness. Seal tightly and place in hot coals. Turn occasionally and cook approximately 25 or 30 minutes.

CHI - bonne' Hamburger

$\frac{1}{2}$ lb. hamburger

2 slices large onion

salt and pepper

1 pat of butter

Grease aluminum foil with butter. Make large hamburger or two small ones. Slice onion on hamburger, salt and pepper and add remaining butter. Wrap and seal tightly and place on coals, onion side up. Turn occasionally. Cook for 15 minutes.

BAKED APPLE

Prepare by taking out core and putting in one half of marshmallow in hole, 2 tsp. brown sugar, one pat of butter, then top with remaining half of marshmallow. Roll in long enough piece of foil to make double thickness. Place in hot coals 10 to 15 minutes.

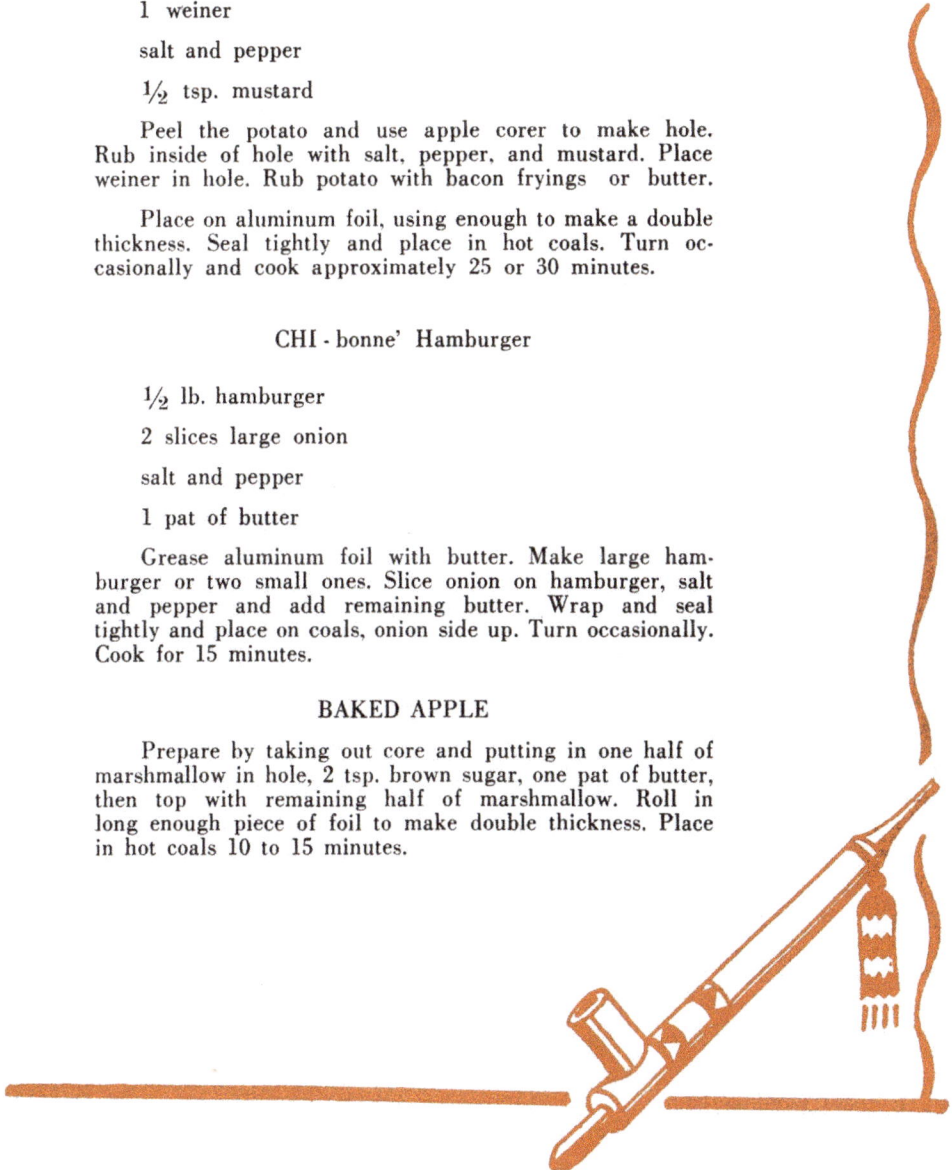

BAKED POTATO (Individual)

1 large potato

butter or bacon fryings.

salt and pepper

Wash potato but do not peel. Make several holes in potato, shake salt and pepper in holes, grease with butter or bacon fryings and then seal in aluminum foil. Place on coals and bake approximately 20 to 25 minutes.

Some of you boys and girls have your mother fix some of these recipes such as, Chi-bonne' hamburger, baked potato, baked apple and wrap them in foil. Put this in a paper sack and when you get to your favorite camping or picnic grounds, build your fire. Let the fire die down to a hot bed of coals, then place your food in the fire. Soon you will have a delicious meal, and better still, no plates to wash or carry home.

These recipes are easy to make, even baby sister can do them. Her name is Sylvia Kathleen.

My grandfather Tinker is always telling me stories about camping in the woods. He told me that most every boy who goes hunting or fishing has at sometime become lost or separated from his companions.

He said the greatest danger in a situation of this kind is allowing yourself to get panicky. The important things to do are, stop, sit-down, think, and above all, remain calm.

It might be well to mention at this point, that you should never leave camp or go for a hunting or fishing trip under any condition without having on your person, a compass, pocket knife, or sheath knife, matches in a water-proof container and a map of the immediate territory in which you are camping.

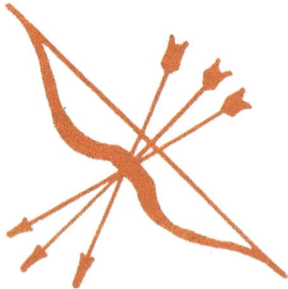

Remember if you are with a party and do not return to camp, they will start a seach for you. Stay put for a day or two and give them a chance to find you. Light a smudge fire as it may be sighted by a Forest Ranger or searchers.

Fire your gun at regular intervals if you have one. If you have a mirror, climb to a high point and flash it, but don't run helter-skelter.

In all sections of our country where there are great expanses of wilderness, expert trackers can be secured. They can find you if you stay in one place, but will never be able to track a person that is panicky, frightened and wanders aimlessly without reason.

In cold weather, start to build yourself a shelter and fire immediately upon finding you are lost. A lost camper can live several days without food if he has the tools necessary to build himself a shelter and a fire. A sheath knife and dry matches will serve to do this in a emergency.

If you keep your head cool and your body warm, you are sure to come out okay.

Starting a fire in wet weather may seem difficult, but it can be done. A little preparation at home before you start on your camping trip will pay off. A few pieces of **paraffin wrapped separately is excellent tinder. Newspapers rolled tightly and dipped in paraffin lengths are also good.**

If you are camping where birch bark is available, it is the best of the natural tinders. A little piece of emery board from a nail file, glued in the top of your water proof match box will give you a dry place to strike your match.

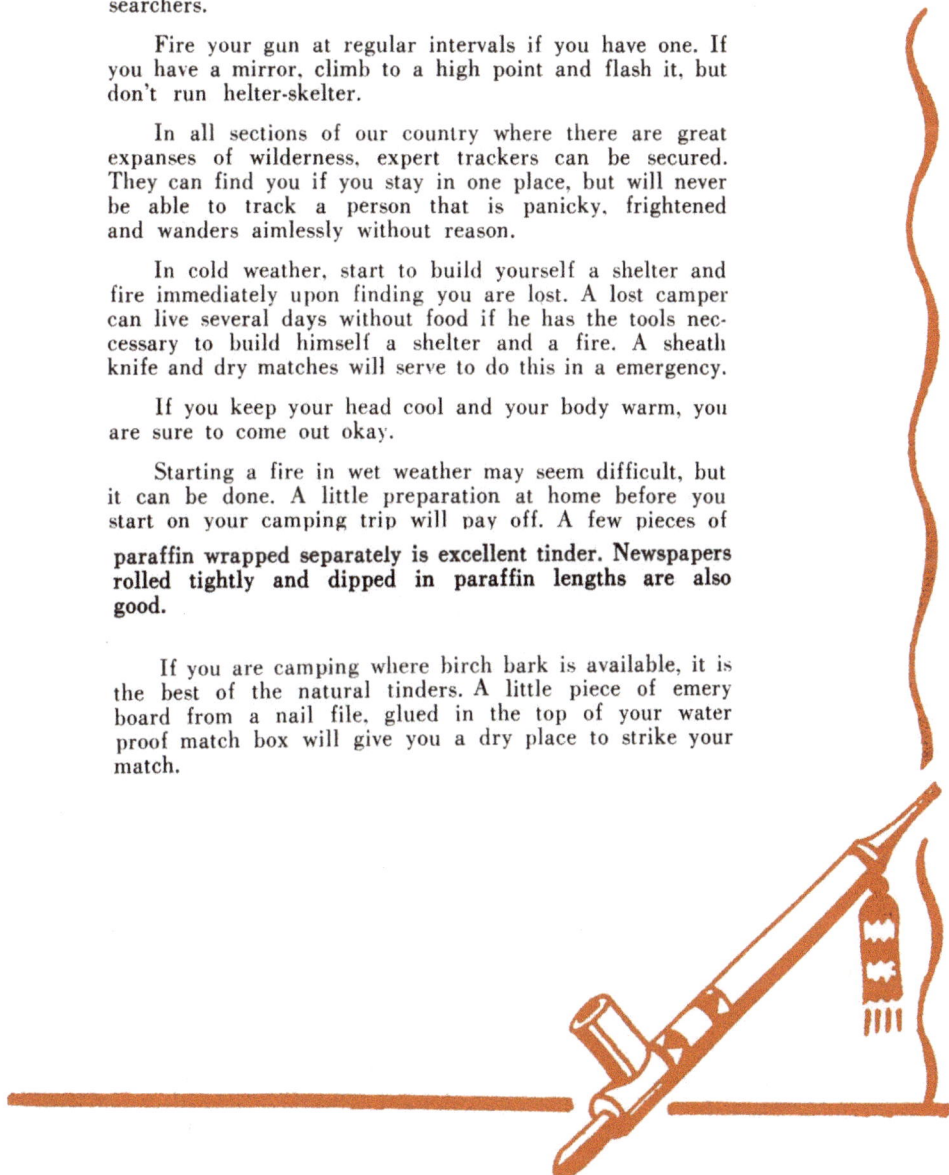

Before attempting to start your fire, gather a good supply of the driest wood you can find. Woods containing a goodly amount of pitch are the best. Dead limbs are also good. It may be necessary to chop into tree stumps or split fallen logs to secure enough fairly dry wood to get your fire started.

The next step is to select a large bunch of the driest twigs and sticks. Place your tinder on the ground on the driest spot obtainable and lay over it some dry shavings, then the twigs and small sticks so they will catch the blaze. As the wood catches fire, more can be added and small split kindlings. Add kindlings gradually, first small sizes then larger, but always split. Do not attempt to add large logs until you have a good, roaring blaze.

In very rainy weather, it may be necessary to shield the small flame with your body, a piece of tarp, or a small lean-to made of boughs and twigs. Once you have a good roaring fire it will take a lot of rain to put it out.

If camping in one spot for any length of time, always keep a supply of kindling in your tent, as it saves time and work.

I hope these hints on cooking, camping out, getting lost in the woods and building a camp fire in rainy weather, will help you when you go camping. My grandfather said every man and boy should know these things.

I hear the big Indian drum beating out a good stomp dance so I will tell you goodbye.

With love
"Shunka" or "Frankie"

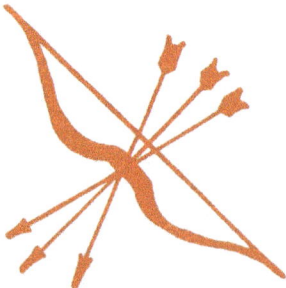

FRANKIE McCLAIN
BACK VIEW INDIAN COSTUME

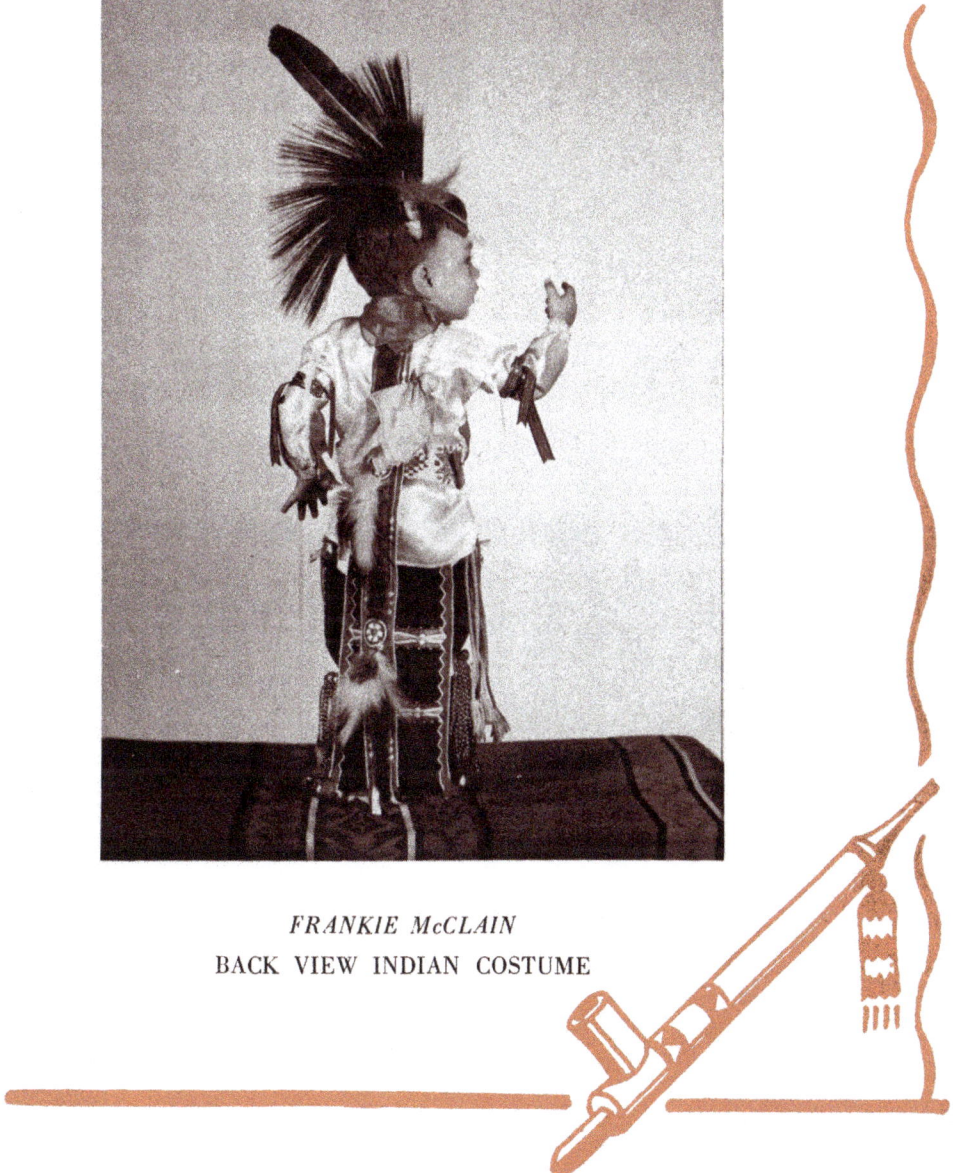

WILD GAME COOKING IS FOR SKILLFUL COOKS

Successful cooking for any wild meat depends on conserving moisture. Game is usually drier and not nearly so fat as domestic meat. The general rule is to cook wild game longer and at even lower temperatures than other meats, and to add fat in some way. For wild ducks, put a few strips of bacon over the breast or spread a coating of fat over the bird and pour a cup of orange juice over it. Baste at least once during cooking time. Roasts of all kinds should be basted frequently. The covered roaster is best for low, slow moist cooking.

Recommended ways for cooking different cuts of venison. Round steak from a young animal is usually tender and can be broiled, from an older animal, it may be tough, but makes delicious Swiss steak. The leg from a young deer is good when roasted whole, as one cooks leg of lamb. Loin, the choicest part of deer, supplies sirloin and porter house steaks, to be cooked as other tender steaks are, or to make tender roasts. The rump makes good pot roasts. The neck, breast and flank are best for stews or ground for "deerburgers," Any of the less tender cuts are delicious when corned.

Quick frozen as you freeze domesticated meat, it provides many future meals.

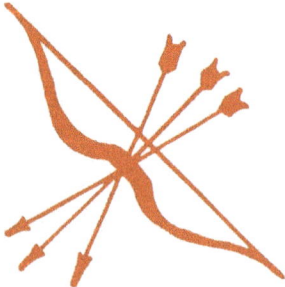

COOKING SMALL GAME

FRIED SQUIRREL

Southern squirrels of the Fox and Grey variety, which feed on hickory nuts acorns and pecans, are among the most delicious small game to be found. It must be remembered, that they differ from the Rocky mountain squirrels which ordinarily are not good for eating.

Young squirrels can be fried just like chicken and the older squirrels are delicious stewed with salt meat, and pepper to taste.

Another method is to stew the squirrel until tender and most of the liquid cooked out. Take one cup of cold coffee and thicken with enough flour to make a paste. Add this to the squirrel broth to make a thick gravy.

BAKED RABBIT

For real delicious eating, take a young rabbit, wild or domestic. Soak in cold water for a few hours. While soaking, make a dressing of 1 pt. bread crumbs, moistened with hot water, 1 tbsp. of meat fryings or butter, 1 tsp. salt, ½ tsp. pepper, 1 tbsp. sage, 1 small onion grated.

If desired par-boil liver and heart. Mince and mix with stuffing. Mix well and fill cavity in rabbit. Rub rabbit with salt, pepper and flour. Add small pieces of salt pork or butter. Bake slowly and baste often until rabbit is tender.

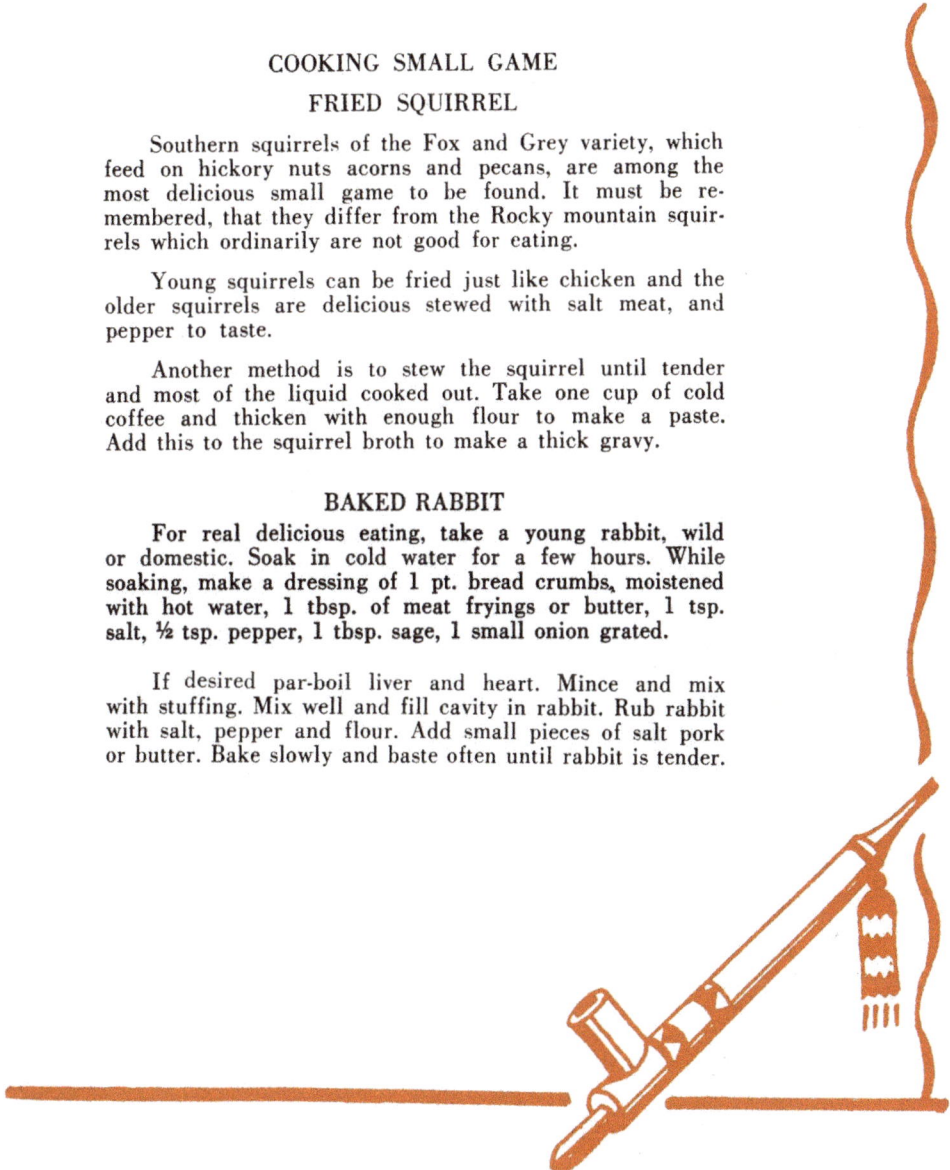

FRIED RABBIT IN BATTER

Cut rabbit in small pieces, put in kettle, salt, cover with water and boil until tender.

Make a batter of 1 cup sour cream or milk, 1/2 tsp. soda 1/8 tsp. salt, 1 egg and 1/2 cup flour. Dip pieces of rabbit in batter and fry in hot fat until golden brown.

RABBIT CUTLETS

Cut rabbit into pieces, simmer until meat is tender, drain and allow to cool. Sprinkle the pieces of rabbit with salt and pepper, dip in flour, beaten egg and crumbs. Fry slowly in butter or shortening until well browned. Then pour over 1 1/2 cups brown sauce, cook slowly over a low flame for 20 to 25 miuntes.

STEWED RABBIT

In a dutch oven or shallow stew pan, Place 2 onions sliced, 2 carrots sliced, 1 bud of minced garlic, 1 cup canned tomatoes, 1 tsp. salt, 1/4 tsp. black pepper and 1/2 tsp. paprika. Add two cups water. Cut up two slices of bacon over it. Cover and simmer until meat is tender, about two hours. Remove the meat and vegetables and thicken broth for gravy.

RABBIT SAUSAGE

Without cooking it, cut as much meat from the bones of a rabbit as can possibly be obtained. Grind the meat with one medium onion, 4 potatoes and one slice of bacon.

Mix well, form into patties, salt and pepper to taste. Dip in cracker crumbs and fry until tender.

BAKED RACOON

Since racoons are wiry and rugged little animals, they require rugged cooking, After cleaning and dressing, par boil the racoon for 30 minutes to an hour. Then place him in a roaster. Dredge with salt and pepper, add medium onion, large carrot and apple. Put in hot water about one to two inches in bottom of roaster. Bake until tender (about two hours), Tomato catsup and mustard may be put on coon while baking or just before removing from oven.

VENISON ROAST

Hind quarter or loin. Wash thoroughly several times in vinegar water and salt. Take one section of garlic, sliced into tiny pieces and spike meat. Place meat in a roaster. cover with heavy sliced bacon. Add two cups hot water. Cover and roast slowly at 300 degrees, approximately 20 minutes per pound. When done prepare mushroom gravy. Slice meat, pour gravy over all and return to oven for about half hour and serve.

CAMP FIRE VENISON

You can cut a long wooden spit, about five feet long from a green willow branch, remove bark, if you do not have an iron spit. Thread the venison steaks on the spit and place on two forked poles driven into the ground. Cook over an open fire that is about two to three feet from the meat. Turn slowly by revolving the spit on poles allowing the meat to brown and sear over uniformly, to seal in the natural flavor of the meat. Chop up two handfuls of parsley and about 4 cloves of garlic and put them into one cup of olive oil. Cut a twig from a tree, wrap a piece of clean cloth around the end of it to make a swab, baste the meat with the olive oil sauce slowly as it cooks. Salt and pepper should be added to suit your taste.

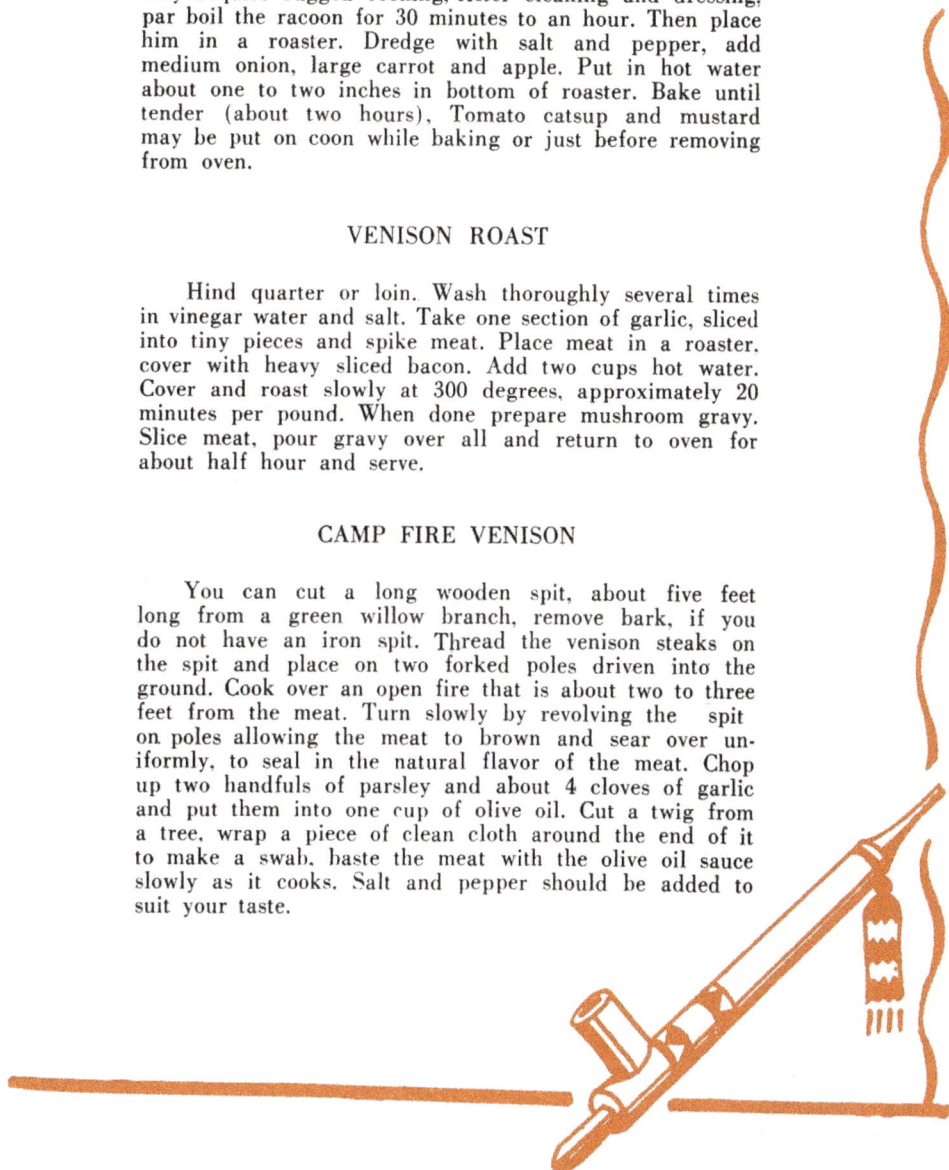

VENISON STEW

Cut your meat up in about 1 inch squares, the amount depending on the number of people to be served. Cut up 3 medium onions, three chili peppers, 3 stalks celery, about a handful parsley minced, a pinch of oregano, Heat cooking oil or olive oil and add these vegetables cooking for about five minutes. Put in the meat, add half cup vinegar to make meat tender. Let fry with the lid on, stirring frequently. The meat will produce its own juice. Cook until it begins to turn white. Next put in two cans of solid pack tomatoes. Now add four or five potatoes cut into inch squares add about same amount chopped carrots. Let this cook for about an hour and a half. Thicken with a little flour and water, one half glass of sherry or claret wine may be added for distinctive flavor. cook in iron pot or dutch oven.

ELK ROAST

Cover roast with salt, pepper, and small amount of garlic salt. Put strips of salt pork on top and brown in hot oven. Add hot water around meat, cover and cook in slow oven 2½ hours. Add sweet potatoes (peeled and halved) and cook for 1½ hours longer. Take potatoes up, thicken gravy. Baste meat with some of the gravy before serving.

BROILED MOOSE STEAK

Take a good steak from the loin. Place it in a wire toaster over a clear fire, turning often. Moose requires more cooking than beef. When sufficiently done, Season with salt and pepper and your favorite steak sauce.

STEAM FRIED STEAK

1½ lbs. round steak, cut in pieces about 1 inch square. Sprinkle with salt, pepper, and roll in flour.

Place in iron (covered) skillet with about 3 tbsps. compound. Sear on both sides, stirring frequently to keep from sticking. When brown add 1½ cups water. Cover and let simmer for about 1 hour. Makes six helpings with thick gravy.

PREPARING BEAR MEAT

Bear steak is best for eating during the early part of the hunting season, especially in areas where bear feed on salmon and other fish since the fish permeates the bear meat. As soon as you have bagged your bear. dress it out immediately, since the hide, entrails and other parts give the meat a strong flavor. Soak it at least over night in cold water before trying to cook it. Prepare and cook bear meat the same as fresh pork in either roasting or frying, making sure to cook it well done since bear meat contains the same elements as pink pork.

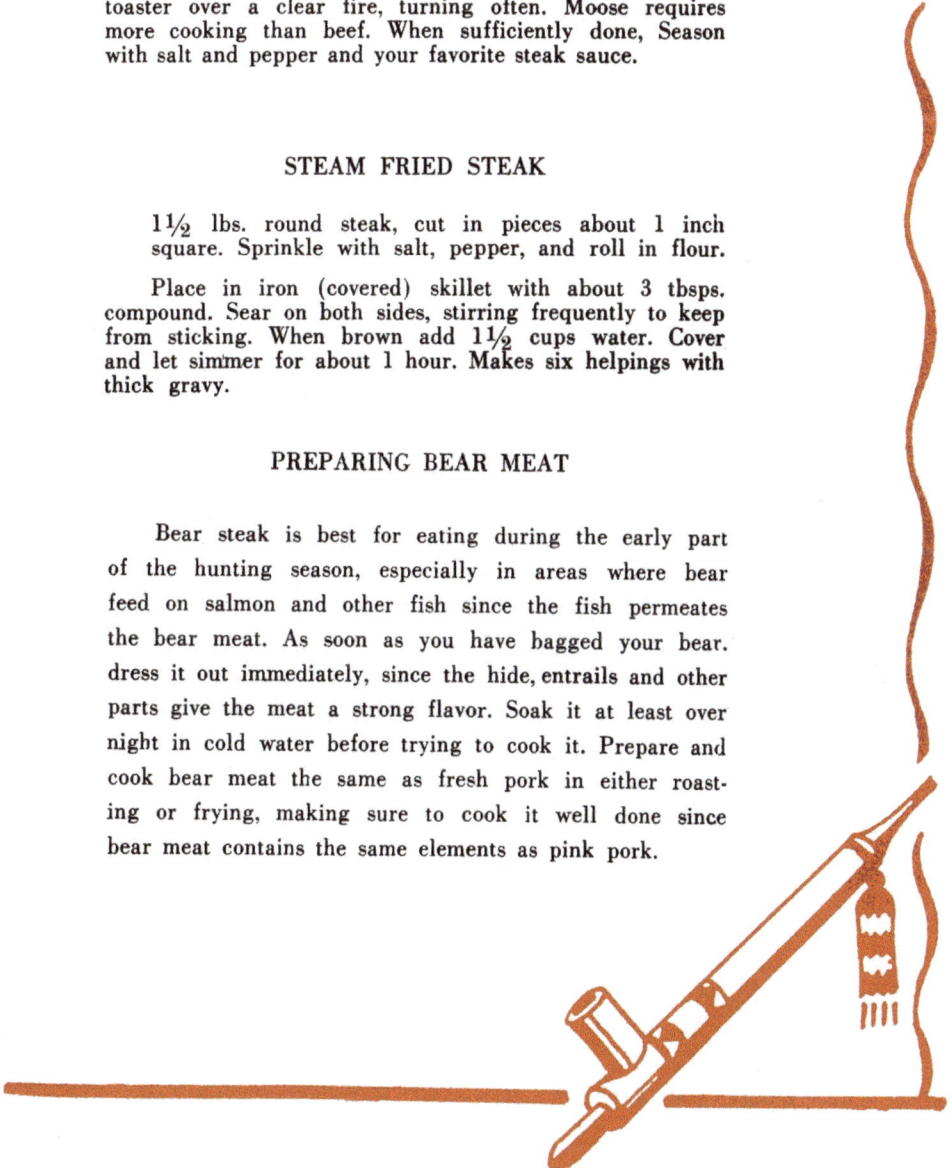

PREPARING GAME BIRDS FOR COOKING

One of the best techniques used in preparing game birds for the roast oven is to slit them down the back, after plucking. As most every one knows, most of the meat on pheasants, wood cock, quail, grouse and other game birds is on the breast. When the birds are slit down the back from the base of the neck to the tail, it will be open for thorough washing and a large amount of stuffing may be inserted in the frame.

You can bind it together with one or two turns of twine and when cooked should lie breast up, allowing for easier carving. Some hunters have the far sight to pick a few wild grapes, beach plums or cranberries if available, to be made into jelly to set off the roasted bird to perfection.

One of the main points to remember when cleaning wild fowl for cooking is to pluck birds (pluck them dry) as quickly as possible after returning from the hunt, and drawing them immediately, washing out the body thoroughly.

To get rid of down feathers on wild ducks, dip them in hot paraffin, after first plucking the big feathers. Be sure to use a large container for dipping. When the paraffin cools, it will be much easier to pull off the down feathers.

FRIED SAGE HEN

This is for young birds only. After you have dressed, cleaned and skinned the bird , soak it in cold water over night. Sprinkle lightly with salt and pepper and dredge with flour. Fry in an iron skillet or heavy aluminum in plenty of grease until golden brown, then pour a little hot water over it and simmer for half an hour or until tender.

QUAIL DELUXE

•

With four quail, you can serve two people a very delicious meal. Just clean the quail as you prepare a turkey to bake (without opening up the back). Place in cold water to chill and prepare stuffing which is made from six slices of toasted bread, one can of oysters, salt and pepper to taste, add hot water to make the dressing as thick as you prefer. After stuffing the birds. bake in an uncovered pan 1½ hours at 350 degrees.

QUAIL WITH RICE

•

Dress and pluck quail, salt and pepper to taste. Dredge with flour and brown on all sides in skillet using melted butter or other shortening. Set quail aside and prepare rice as follows.

Wash rice well and drain dry, through a colander. Cut up two good sized onions, one stalk of celery three long chili or bell peppers, 6 sprigs parsley and a bit of garlic. Heat a frying pan and add a good film of cooking oil, olive or wesson oil, approximately 3 tbsp. Add well drained rice and cook, stirring constantly until rice turns a golden brown. Add the cut up vegetables to the rice, adding a little more oil if needed. Continue cooking until vegetables are tender, stirring frequently. Add one large can solid pack tomatoes, and let simmer for 15 minutes. Add a good big pinch of oregano (at times called Mexican sage), then put in the quail whole, and cover with a well fitting lid. Allow to cook over slow heat until rice is done. This should take about 30 minutes. Add salt and pepper to taste. Do not stir after adding quail.

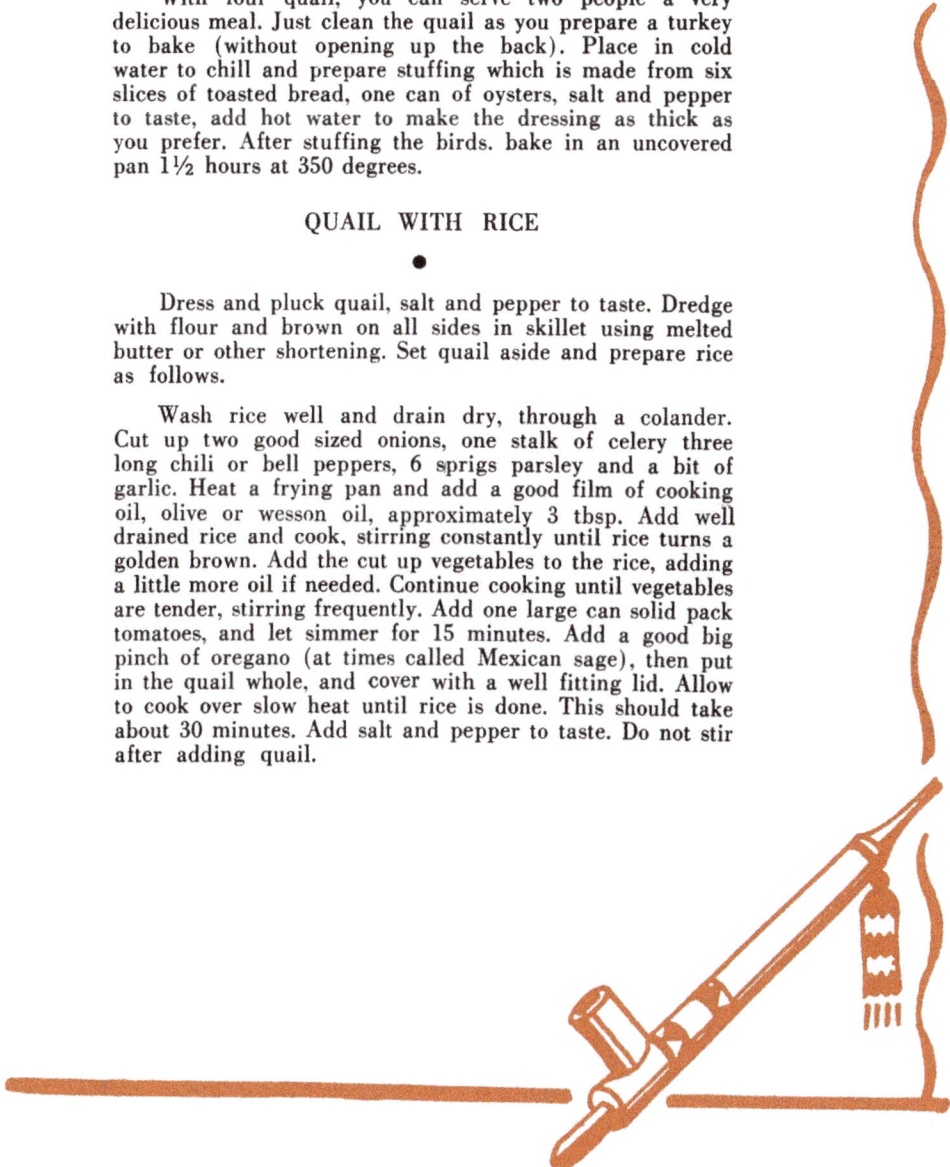

WILD DUCK POT ROAST

Sear each duck in hot fat until brown all over. Put in pan 1 tbsp. lard, 1 tbsp. whole mixed spices, 1 onion and a few stalks of celery cut fine. Add 1 cup hot water, cover tightly and cook slowly 3 hours. Add hot water as needed. Add a dash of red pepper and make a gravy with remaining liquor, then run through a sieve and serve.

ROAST WILD DUCK WITH DRESSING

After cleaning and dressing duck, rub with salt about 1 tsp. per pound of fowl. Brown lightly in two tablespoons of butter or shortening. Place duck on steamer rack in roaster, using dripping to make dressing. Pour dressing over duck and garnish with onions, stuffed olives and slices of hard boiled egg. Add one cup boiling water to roaster, bake 2 hours at 400 degrees.

DRESSING FOR DUCK

1 chopped onion, 1 cup stale bread crumbs, 1 cup cracker crumbs; ½ cup corn bread crumbs; ½ tsp. each of salt, pepper and sage and celery salt. Add drippings and 1 cup boiling water, then beat in three eggs, one at a time, 1 cup chopped celery or chestnuts may be added if desired.

WILD DUCK

Split young wild duck down the back and rub with olive oil or butter (melted). Dust with salt and pepper, broil about 20 to 30 minutes.

Black currant jelly, squares of fried hominy grit, and a green salad, with dressing, goes well with duck. To make dressing, soak two buds of garlic cut in half, in a half cup of vinegar for three days. Remove garlic, add three cups of salad oil, and one can of tomato soup. Salt and pepper to taste. Mix well. This dressing will keep indefinitely in the refrigerator in closed jar or bottle.

ROAST DUCK

Dress the duck, leaving skin on. Rub lightly with olive oil and season with salt and pepper. Moisten fresh bread crumbs in sweet milk for stuffing and add seasoning to taste. Stuff the duck and roast until almost done.

Place two slices of tart apples and two slices of oranges with peel, on each duck. Finish roasting. Thicken drippings with flour to make thin sauce, then strain and add 4 oz. red wine. Serve with candied orange or pickled crab apples.

BAKED WILD TURKEY

Let the dressed turkey hang for a night or two in the frosty air. Disjoint and wash thoroughly, turn in well seasoned flour and brown in bacon fat or other frying fat in a dutch oven, until well browned. Add a little water, cover oven and heap with hot coals, banking down so that coals will hold the heat. For a young bird, cook about 3 hours. Larger ones should be cooked longer, and coals kept hot.

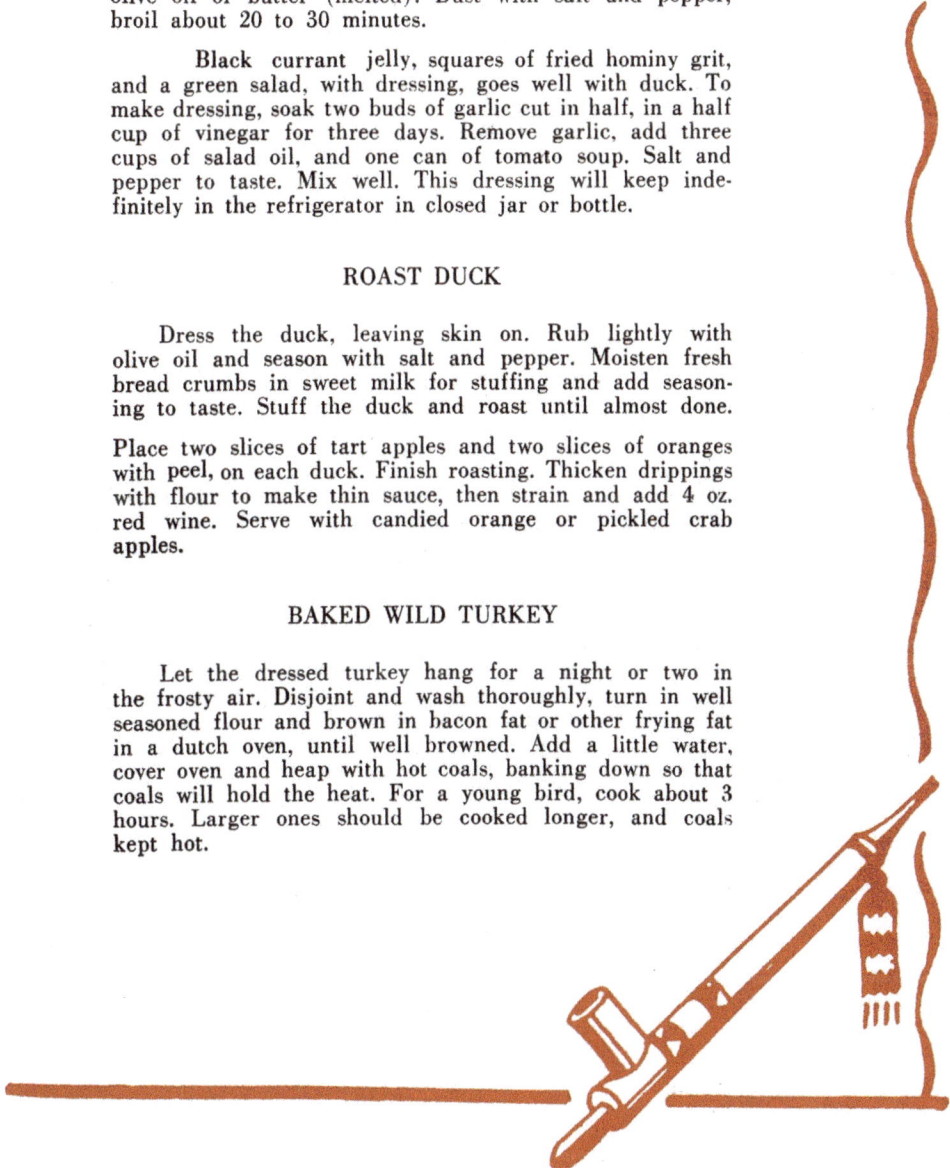

BAKED PHEASANT OR PEA HEN

Pheasant should be scalded, plucked and drawn. Thorough chilling is necessary. Cover the dressed pheasant with damp cloth and place in refrigerator over night. It is not necessary to freeze it.

Disjoint and cut the pheasant up in same manner as fried chicken, but leave leg and second joint together.

Mix salt, pepper and flour together, using about 1 tbsp. salt, $\frac{1}{2}$ tsp. black pepper and 1 cup flour. Roll each piece in the mixture, brown on all sides in a skillet in melted butter.

After browning each portion, remove to a heavy aluminum or iron roaster which bakes on a top burner. Turn gas on low as possible and add a little water from time to time to prevent burning. Cook at least $2\frac{1}{2}$ hours. Almost as good results can be obtained by using an oven roaster. Cooking as slowly as possible.

FRICASSEE OF PHEASANT

Pluck pheasants for best results. Draw them, then cut into convenient pieces for frying, removing any short torn meat. Wipe clean with damp cloth. Fry to a golden color in fat consisting of $\frac{3}{4}$ shortening to $\frac{1}{3}$ butter. If all butter is used it will burn easily. Add a little water from time to time, dusting the gravy lightly with flour from a shaker. Salt and pepper to suit your own taste. Add more butter from time to time if you like. When the pheasant is tender and the gravy rich and thick, transfer to oven casserole and just about half cover with rich cream. Cook on a moderate oven until the cream has blended with the gravy and evaported some what.

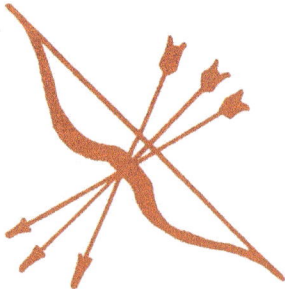

COOKING FISH

It is usually better for wild game to be hung up and aged for a few days before it is cooked, but fish is best if cooked and eaten shortly after being caught. Where it is not to be eaten immediately it should be kept in the

best possible condition. Fish that must be carried considerable distances, especially in hot weather, should be cleaned as soon as possible, wiped dry and placed between layers of leaves, ferns, paper or cloth to prevent them touching each other. Exposure to sun or moisture will cause the fish to spoil quickly.

To clean fish, split belly from head to vent, remove insides and scrape clot of blood from the back bone, trim off fins and remove scales by holding fish by the tail and scraping with a knife or fish scaler, toward the head. Brook trout need to be scraped only enough to remove the slime. For appearance sake, small fish are sometimes cooked without removing the head or tail, and the same is true of larger fish in some ways of cooking, but they are easier cleaned if they are removed. Wash inside and out with cold water and wipe dry with paper toweling or clean cloth.

Usually small fish are fried in a pan while the larger ones are prepared in other ways. To fry a small fish, sever the back bone to prevent curling and sprinkle with salt and pepper. Place fat or shortening in a heavy skillet. I use more shortening than most people do, (about ⅓ full). Put fish in hot fat and brown first one side then the other, over very hot coals. Then reduce the heat some-what and cook 5 to 10 minutes more.

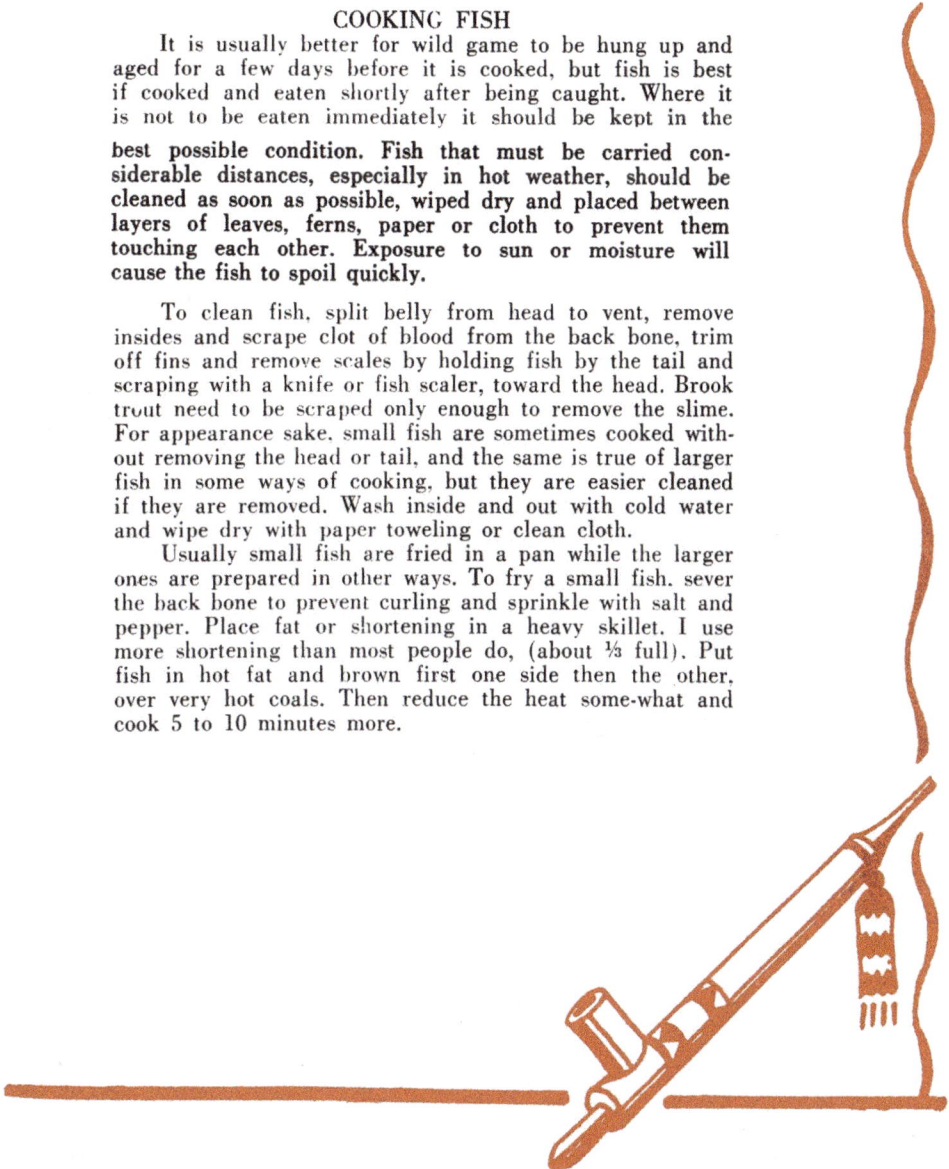

Remember the fat you use for frying the fish should be very hot or the flesh will become soggy by absorbing it.

Some people like to dip their fish in cornmeal, flour crumbs or a mixture of cornmeal and flour. I use cornmeal mixed with flour, about three parts cornmeal and one part flour. Good fats to use include butter, bacon drippings, pork fat or vegetable shortening. You can cook fish any number of ways, broiling, boiling, baking, frying and smoking.

If you catch an especially large fish, you may want to have it mounted, and here is how you prepare it for the taxidermists. Most taxidermists prefer to receive a fish unskinned in order that they may make a cast of the same very often this is impossble. After catching your fish you want to have mounted, place it on a paper and mark carefully around it with a pencil making an accurate outline and also the size and individual shape.

Write down notes as to color as it fades rapidly.

To reproduce this specimen, the taxidermist must know these details.

After making the outline and notes, the fish is prepared as follows: Cut open the side, not the belly, preserving the perfect side. Take off skin carefully. Most skin will peel off easily. Fins should be separated at the base from the body with a sharp knife or scissors. Scrap off grease with a spoon. Skin should be spread and rubbed with salt on the inner side only and let lay for 24 hours. The following day, roll up in a piece of paper and store in a box or tin can with air holes for ventilation. The specimen will keep for several days until ready to ship for mounting. Be sure to enclose notes and sketch with shipment.

FRIED TROUT OR OTHER FISH

Salt fish generously and dip in cornmeal and flour mixture. Have fat deep and hot. Cook fish until brown, turn and brown other side. Small fish should be cooked fast like French fried potatoes, larger one's more slowly after browning them. Turn heat up before taking up so they will be crisp. Drain on brown paper towel. Most fish can be fried in this way.

BROILED FISH

One of the best ways to broil fish is to place them in the broiler, clean and dry, sprinkle with salt and pepper. If the fish is large, it may be cut in slices and turned quite often, or it may be cut along the back bone instead of the belly, laying it open like a book, placed flesh side down on the broiler then turned and cooked on the outside.

BROILED TROUT

Split trout open so they will be flat. Remove bones and dust with salt, pepper and garlic salt. Dot with salt pork and broil under slow flame until slightly brown. Broil approximately 20 minutes for small trout and 30 minutes for larger ones.

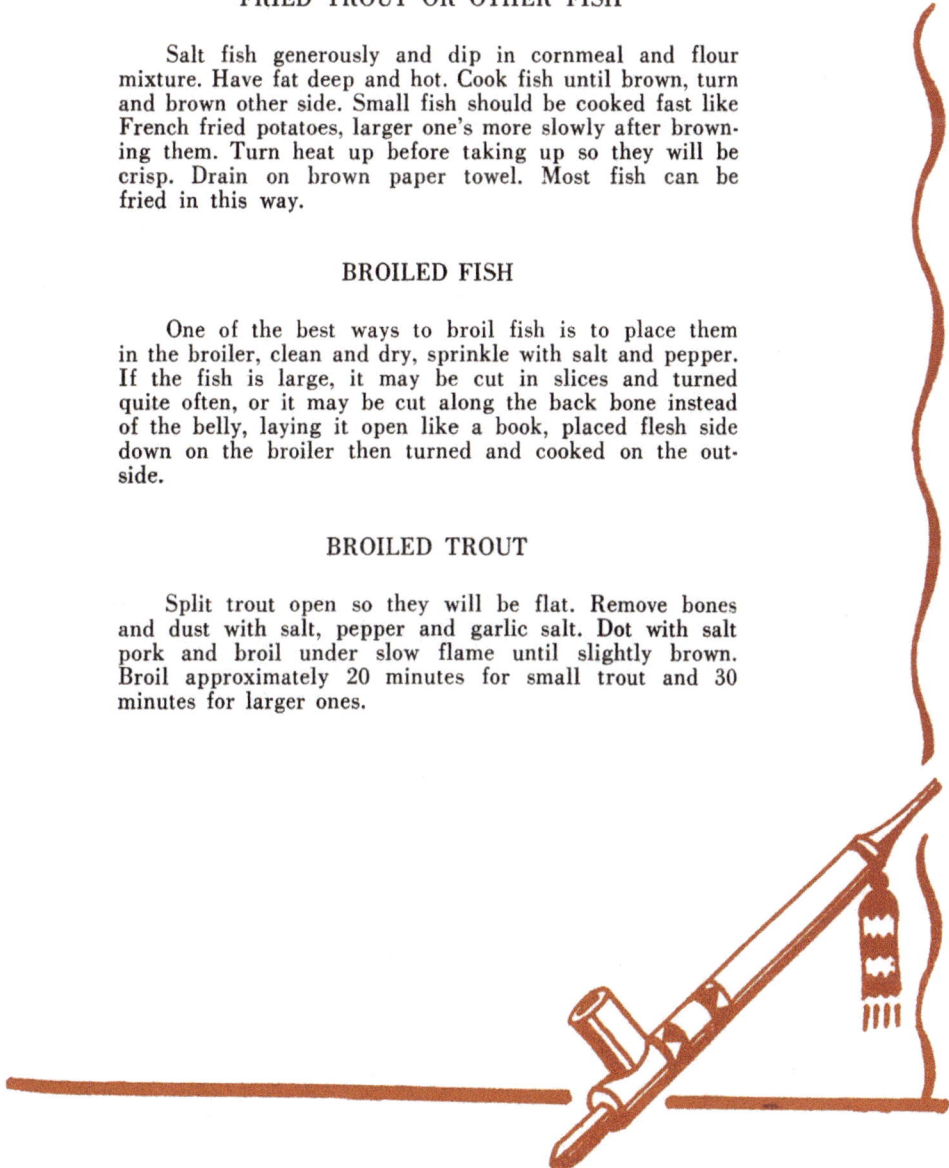

SMOKED FISH

Many out door men find it helpful in keeping trout or other fish preserved for several weeks by smoking them, which makes them good eating from the hand, like smoked herrings.

Trout over 9 inches and under 12 inches are easily smoked. Salt the trout first and allow them to drip. To build a smokey fire use slightly punky hardwood, beech, birch or soft maple.

Build a rack with four corners with sticks driven into the ground and cover the rack with green whips. Leaving room for smoke to curl all around them. The whole rack may be enclosed with ever green thatch. From 2 to 6 hours smoking is ample to cure them, depending on size.

BOILED FISH

For boiling fish only those of fairly large size, three pounds or more, should be used. Clean fish and wrap in clean cheese cloth, place in salted boiling water. Boil gently until flesh easily separates from the bones.

It takes 8 to 10 minutes per pound on boiling large fish and about 5 minutes per pound for smaller fish. Drain well and season with butter or white sauce.

BAKED TROUT

Dust fish with salt, pepper and garlic salt. Fill inside with onion, green pepper and celery cut fine. Put strips of salt pork on top and brown in oven. Cover and cook until tender in slow oven about one hour.

Bread dressing can be used if desired.

BAKED WALL-EYED PIKE

After scaling fish and cutting off the head, slit down the back and crosswise on each side. Put slice of fat pork in side slits and salt the fish inside and out.

Make a dressing of moistened bread crumbs, 1/4 lb. of salt pork, chopped fine. Place into the fish cavity, fasten with toothpicks. Line pan with thin strips of fresh side pork. Bake in moderate oven until tender. Baste frequently with milk. If you wish to bake this fish over a camp fire, place strips of pork on aluminum foil. Roll fish in this, forming two thicknesses of the foil. Seal tightly and place on bed of hot coals and turn frequently. Omit basting. About one hour for baking, depending on size.

BAKED BASS STUFFED

After the bass have been cleaned and skined, spread thin strips of salt pork in a baking pan and lay the fish over them. Stuff the cavity with dressing and spread the remaining dressing on top of the fish then lay slices of salt pork over the fish. Cover bottom of pan with one inch of milk. Bake in moderate oven until nicely browned. Baste frequently with pan gravy.

DRESSING FOR FISH

Four slices of white bread broken into pieces, 2 stalks of celery cut fine, small onion grated, 1 medium sized carrot grated, 1 tbsp. minced green pepper, 2 tbsp. chopped cabbage, 1 tbsp. butter, 1 beaten egg, 1/2 tbsp. poultry seasoning, 1 tsp. salt, 1 tbsp. mayonaise, Mix and add boiling water until of consistency to spread.

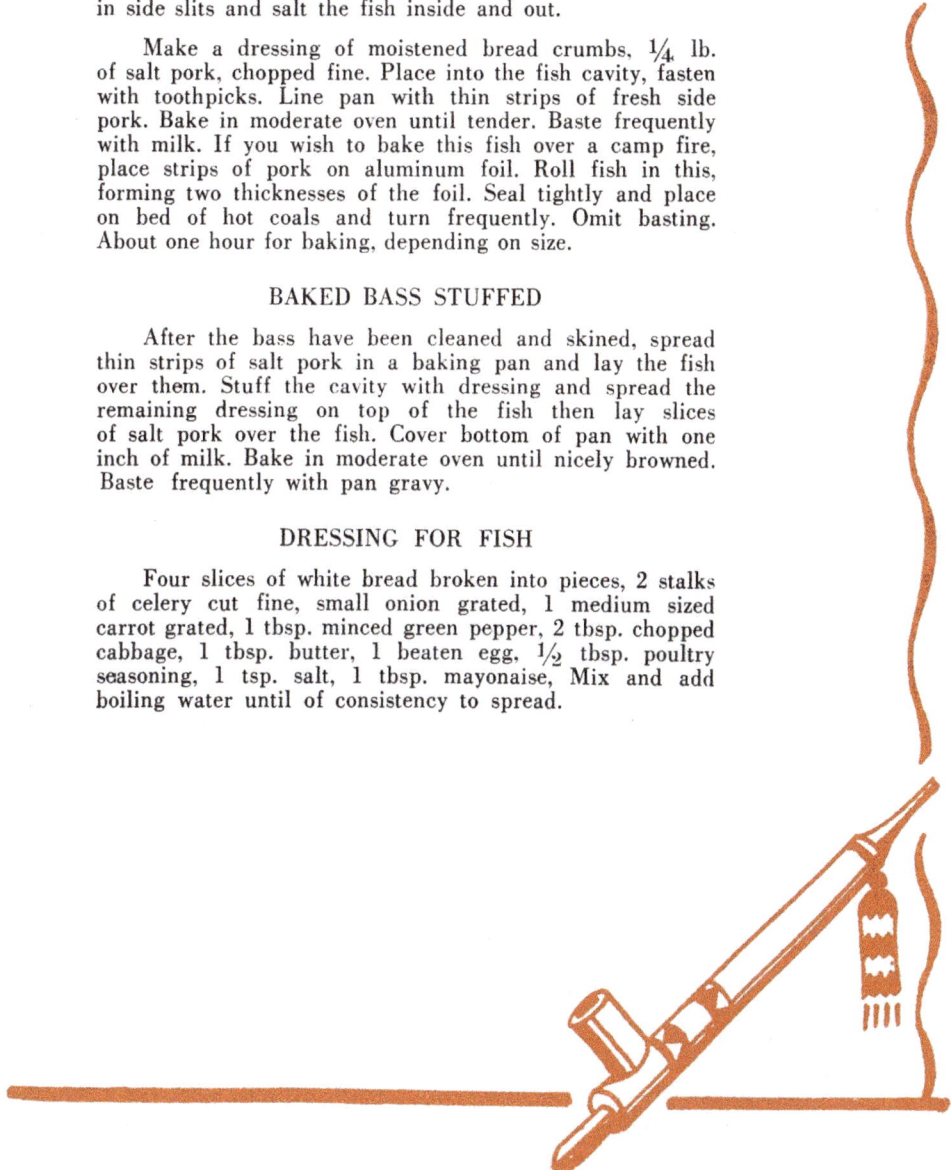

CAMP RECIPES

SOUR DOUGH BREAD
●

2 cups flour

2 tbsp. of sugar

1 tsp. salt

Mix with sufficient water to form a thin batter and set in a warm place to sour. This takes about 48 hours. Don't worry about the odor. it will be taken care of in the baking. When thoroughly sour, add 1 tsp. baking soda and enough flour to make a stiff dough. Knead into small loaves or biscuits and set in warm place to rise. When about double the original size, they are ready to bake. 350 degrees for about 25 minutes.

Make biscuits and place in greased dutch oven set in warm place near campfire until double in size. Turn over now and then so they will not be too hot or raise too fast. When doubled in size bake in dutch oven over hot coals.

DUTCH OVEN BATTER BREAD
●

2 cups of flower

1 tsp. sugar

3 tsp. Baking Powder

1½ (approximately) cups cold water

¼ cup melted shortening

Mix dry ingredients thoroughly. Stir in cold water, mixing rapidly to make a thick batter that will pour out evenly. Have dutch oven ready with ¼ cup melted shortening. Pour batter in dutch oven, cover and bake on bed of coals.

CAMP FIRE CHICKEN
(Foil Wrapped)

2 slices bacon

chicken drum stick, (or equivalent)

1 large potato

1 pat butter

salt and pepper to taste

½ carrot, turnip or any desired vegetable

Wash chicken and vegetables. Take about 25 or 30 inch sheet of aluminum wrap. Place bacon on wrap, chicken on top. Slice vegetables ¼ inch slices on top of chicken, place butter for seasoning then top with remaining slice of bacon. Fold to seal as tightly as possible, without breaking the foil. Place on hot bed of coals. Bake 15 minutes, turn and bake 15 minutes more. Should be done in 30 minutes.

CAMP FIRE STEAK
(Foil Wrapped)

1 tbsp. butter	1 lb. steak
salt and pepper	2 carrots
1 large potato	1 onion

Take about 30 inches of aluminum foil, wash and peel vegetables, also wash steak for added moisture. Spread butter on bottom of wrap. Place steak over it. Slice potatoes over steak, slice onion, thin, over potatoes, and slice carrots and place on each side of steak.

Fold up foil lengthwise. Make the seal. Place on hot coals for 20 to 25 minutes, turning after half of cooking time.

Prepare individual packages of above portions at home before going on picnic or camping trip. Keep in small ice box until ready to be cooked.

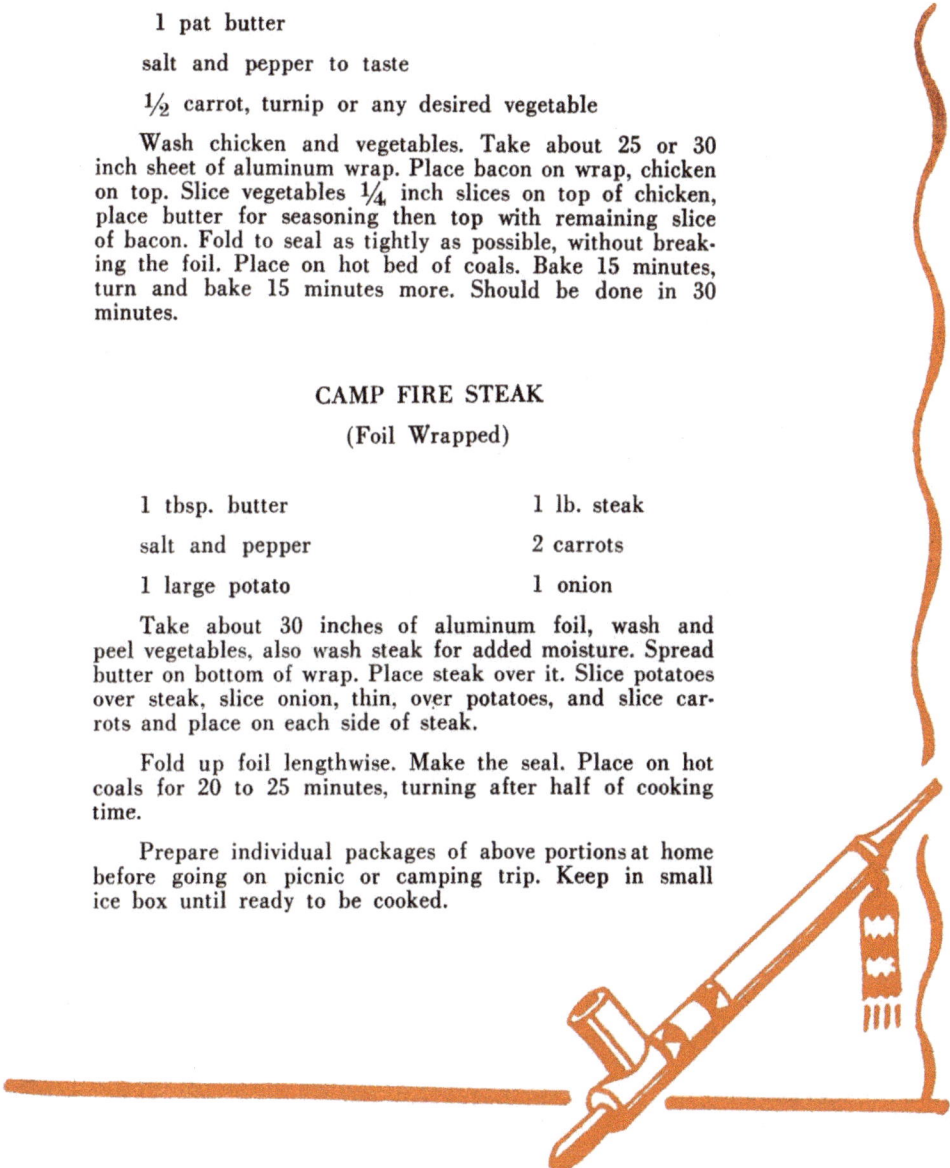

DRIED FRUITS

●

Dried fruits are especially good for campers. They take up smaller space than canned fruits and are easy to prepare.

Cooking dried fruits. Rinse and cover with water. Let soak over night and then simmer in the same water for a few minutes or until tender.

Use $\frac{1}{4}$ or $\frac{1}{2}$ cup of sugar for each cup of fruit, depending on sweetness desired.

Prunes and apricots are very good for a camp fire meal.

BOILED RICE CAMPFIRE STYLE

●

Wash $\frac{1}{2}$ cup rice in cold water and drain. Pour slowly into 1 qt. of rapidly boiling water, salted with 1 tsp. salt. Cook for 20 minutes without stirring. Drain off any excess water and hang pot high over fire without cover, for rice to swell and dry.

RICE PATTIES

●

Mix cooked rice with beaten eggs and form into patties. Fry in hot grease until golden brown and serve with syrup and butter. Left over rice can be used in this way.

DAUGHTERS OF CHIEF PAUL REDEAGLE
OF THE OSAGE TRIBE OF INDIANS

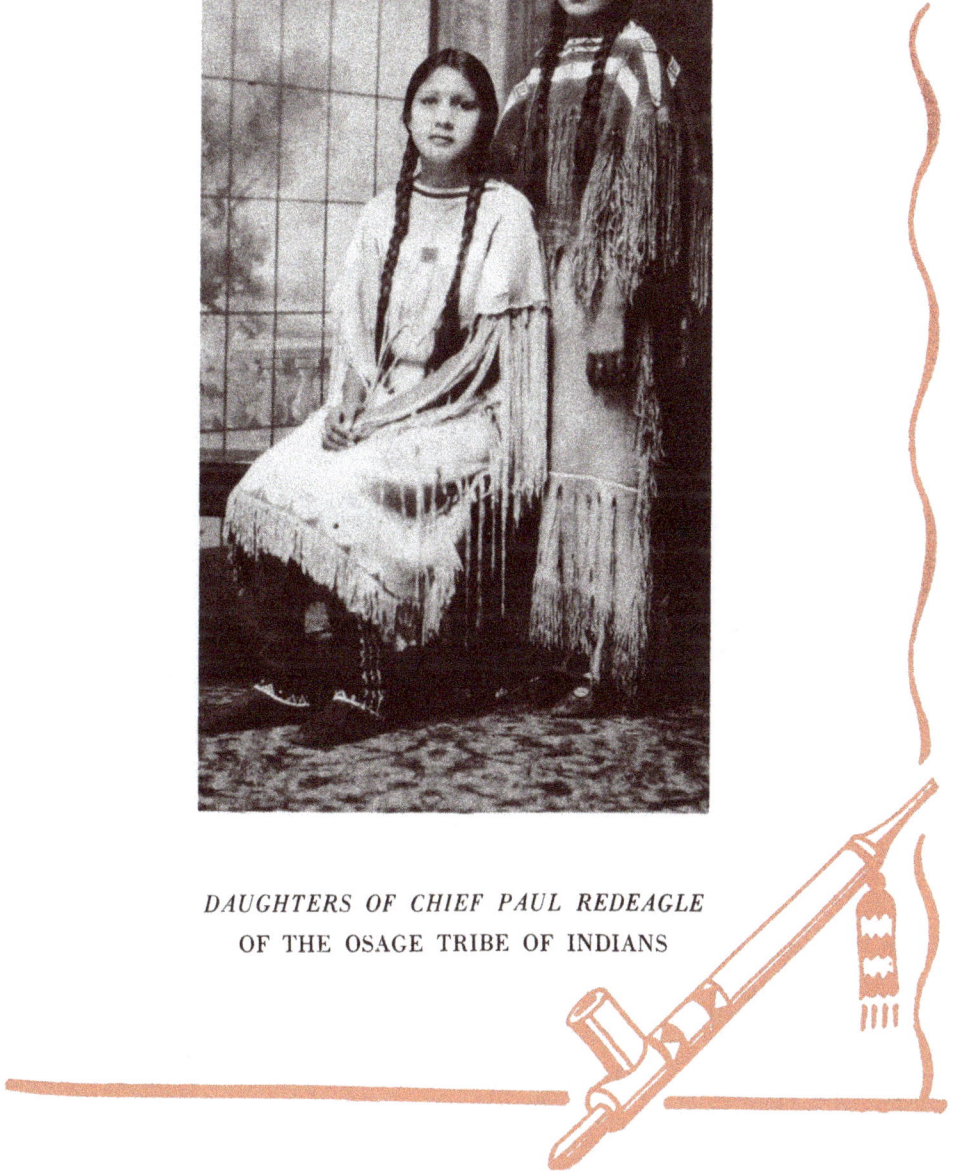

SOME SUGGESTIONS ON OUT-DOOR COOKING
WITH ALUMINUM FOIL

Never use a flaming fire. A bed of hot coals is the thing.

Always add shortening, butter, fat or bacon, also all seasonings, salt and pepper, etc., before wrapping to cook.

Cooking time will vary with type of fire wood, wind strength and many other factors.

It is a good idea to turn package when contents are half done to insure even cooking.

Package will have to be crimped carefully for complete sealing to keep in juices, to assure steam cooking.

Place food to be cooked on a sheet of foil. The sheet should be big enough to allow for a three fold crimping of open edges.

Make an air tight envelope by folding in half and crimp the three open edges. Make three folds on these edges.

Take another sheet of foil the same size as first sheet, repeat folding and crimping, making a double thickness around the food.

Place the packages directly on prepared bed of coals. When food is half done turn, after cooking time is completed open crimped edges, turn back and you have serving dishes, doing away with dirty pots and dishes to wash.

The modern way of cooking over campfires with aluminum foil, would put the Indian cook to shame.

After a hard day of whipping the stream or tramping the woods, have you ever returned to camp to find a pile of greasy, smoky black pots and kettles waiting to be scoured? Or, have you ever awakened in the early dawn to meet the mess of the night before? You left the cooking utensils unwashed, so now, before the meal can be prepared, the pots must be scrubbed out and the frying pan scoured clean. It is unpleasant working and it takes time, so if you can't get your squaw to come along to do dishes and cook on the next trip get several boxes of aluminum foil.

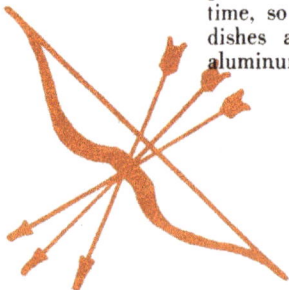

OKLAHOMA

Indian Cook Book

THE BEST INDIAN RECIPES
FROM THE BEST INDIAN STATE

ABOUT THE AUTHOR

An adventuring young man from Tennessee came to the Indian Territory to sell lightning rods to the early settlers. George Lee Wadley met a beautiful Choctaw-Chickasaw Indian girl, married her and decided to stay in the new Indian country.

Wadley and his young bride located at Tamaha on the banks of the Arkansas in eastern Indian Territory; he was appointed U. S. mail carrier. Later he went into business, owning a General Merchandise Store. The entire town turned out with festival spirit on the days when the steamboat docked on its run from Fort Smith up the Arkansas River, bringing supplies for the merchants and mail for the people.

Truly Americana, and in this rich historic and picturesque background of early Oklahoma, the Wadleys were blessed with ten children. Mrs. Wadley soon became highly praised, by friends and neighbors, for her wonderful cooking. Her daughter, Mae, was always by her side in the kitchen, because Mae shared her mother's love and interest in "good cooking," and was anxious to learn all that her mother could teach her. Ever, since those early days, Mae Wadley Abbott has made an art of cooking and her really good American food is a glorious praise to her mother.

Foreword

Food is: The most classifying of any one thing as to racial edification according to anthropologists.

As an American Indian woman, I have realized that Indian Foods, like the Mystic, Ceremonial and Religious Phases of the Red Man is fast disappearing into the past; since food did constitute a very important part in the background of the Indian and history of this American Continent, I became desirous to record some of the best Indian recipes. Therefore, I started compiling a collection of these recipes—some I know; others, I acquired by going out into the beautiful hills and plains of Oklahoma, contacting Indian women and by word of mouth getting many recipes of favorite Indian Food and how to prepare it.

The older Indian Women are passing on; a few years hence and they will have taken to their graves the secrets that are valuable, both as history and aid to those of the future who desire knowledge of how to cook Indian Food.

I have selected fifty-seven of the best recipes for this book in honor of the Mid-Centennial of Oklahoma—the Fiftieth Birth Year of our State.

I herewith offer you Fifty-Seven of the Best American Indian Recipes for 1957.

Hope You Enjoy Them!

MAE WADLEY ABBOTT
Choctaw Roll Number 7559

INDIAN DISHES

These two Indian dishes were contributed by Mr. and Mrs. John Gates of Fort Yates, North Dakota. Mr. Gates' grandfather was Chief Two-Bear of the Sioux Indians.

WECEMIZE WESNE

4 cups parched corn, ground fine

1 cup suet

2 cups dried wild choke cherries

Mix well together, let stand until firm, and slice for use as dessert.

DAKOTA WESHUNGLE

4 dried cow hoofs	2 cups dried pumpkin
2 cups Indian sweet corn	3 pounds fresh short ribs
1 cup wild prairie turnips	2 teaspoons salt

1 teaspoon black pepper

Cook cow hoofs over slow fire about 4½ hours. Add other ingredients about 2 hours before serving.

Mr. and Mrs. Watie Pettit, Cherokees, of Wichita, Kansas kindly contributed the following group of recipes. Mr. Pettit was editor of the former NEW CHEROKEE ADVOCATE published in Tahlequah, Oklahoma.

ASH LYE

Burn black jack wood to ashes. Place in cloth sack and pour boiling water through ashes draining water into a pan.

This lye was used for making hominy and also for making soap.

LYE DUMPLINGS

Sift about 4 cups meal with 1 teaspoon soda and 1 teaspoon salt. Stir in boiling water until dough will hold its shape when moulded. Cook covered in boiling water until done. Soda turns the meal yellow like lye.

Can be served with fried or boiled pork.

DRYING MELONS AND PUMPKINS

Pick best melons, peel, take out seeds, and cut in slices to be strung on sticks. Put them in the sun to dry turning often. When strips are dry, string and hang them in the house to store.

Pumpkins are dried in the same manner.

DRYING CORN

Take good roasting ears and cut kernels from cob. Spread on a clean sheet and dry in the hot sun 3 or 4 days. Store in cloth sacks. My favorite Indian food, cooked with hog jowls.

INDIAN CORN BREAD

1 quart corn meal

Add boiling water enough to make it **stick together**, form into loaf and **bake 1 hour.**

BEAN BREAD (for family of 6 or 8)

2 pounds shelled beans

4 cups meal sifted well with salt, soda, and baking powder

1 level teaspoon salt

1 level teaspoon soda

1 rounded teaspoon baking powder

Cook beans about half done in water enough that it will be about 1½ inches over beans. Do not use any seasoning in the beans. Pour beans scalding hot over meal, soup and all. If the dough is not soft enough with the bean soup add boiling water untol dough will hold its shape when moulded into cakes or pones. For dumplings, shape dough into round balls and drop into boiling water, cook covered until done. For bread, mould into oblong loaves, bake in greased pan, or mould into flat round cakes, wrap in corn shucks or hickory leaves, drop into boiling water, and cook covered until done.

SWEET POTATO BREAD

Same as bean bread except that you use the potatoes raw. Dice about 6 large sweet potatoes, put them in the meal, and add boiling water to make a dough that will hold its shape when made into cakes. Make round cakes, wrap in corn shucks or hickory leaves, drop into boiling water, and cook until done.

INDIAN CORN LIGHT BREAD

3 pints rye meal

3 pints Indian meal (yellow corn meal)

2 tablespoons salt

3 tablespoons shortening

1 teaspoon soda

1 cup thick molasses

2 cakes yeast

Dissolve yeast in ½ cup luke warm water, scald the meal with 1 pint hot water and let cool. When luke warm add all the remaining ingredients and let rise until double in bulk. Knead and form into loaves. It is much nicer baked in individual pans. Let rise 2 hours and bake at 450 degrees for 15 minutes, then reduce to 350 degrees for 30 minutes, making a total of 45 minutes baking time.

SOUR CORN BREAD

Take ½ gallon of sofkey grits. Soak over night. Next morning drip dry in cloth sack and pound or grind into meal.

Mix as for corn bread, salt, soda, baking powder, ½ cup flour, and the powdered grits. Let stand in a warm place for 8 hours, pour into a greased skillet and bake.

RAISED CORN BREAD

Take about 4 cups corn meal, sift and stir in luke warm water until a stiff dough is formed. Leave it in the bowl in a warm place to rise. This takes from a day to a day and a half. When it has raised, break it up, add soda, salt, 2 tablespoons sugar, and 1 egg.

If dough is too stiff add buttermilk to soften. Put in greased baking pans, let rise again, and bake.

WILD GREENS

Gather and clean poke, lamb's quarter, dandelion, and dock. Cook salt pork until tender, add greens and cook until they are tender.

CORN AND BEANS

To skin corn take hot wood ashes, put together with corn in iron pot over open fire, pour water over mixture and stir to crack the skin. When the skin has cracked pour more water over the corn to cool it, wash it very thoroughly through several waters to remove the lye. Rub off the skin.

When the corn is clean, put in pot, cover with water, and cook until about half done, add the beans and cook until both are tender. Serve hot or cold, or fry in grease to serve. Beaten walnut halves added to this and served with sugar or salt is a fine combination. Corn may be completely cooked and used by itself also.

PARCHED CORN

Parch corn in hot ashes until brown. Sift ashes out of corn and beat until a grit stage is reached. Sift meal until nothing but the grits are left, add grits to hot water to make a soup to suit your taste.

Hunters often carried parched meal on long trips instead of rations. It made a very filling food, as about a handful is enough for a meal.

DRYING CORN

Cut top ¾ of kernels off cob of roasting ears. Spread fresh uncooked corn on cheese cloth stretched on a frame and put in sun to dry. Turn corn about 4 times a day and dry until all juice has been evaporated and kernels have become very hard. Store in a bag or an earthen jar with a cover in a dry place.

To cook dried corn, take as much as you desire to serve, cover with an inch of water, salt to taste, season with any meat seasoning and cook until done. This is delicious with fresh pork dishes. Dried corn will keep indefinitely.

PIG'S FEET AND HOMINY

Take 12 fresh pig's feet, cook until meat falls off the bone. When half cooked add 1 gallon of hominy and 2 dried red peppers, and cook down until it thickens. Salt to taste.

WILD ONIONS AND EGGS

Take about 4 bunches of wild onions and cook in bacon grease, salt, and a little water. Cook until tender. Add six eggs and scramble. Serve hot.

This is a popular dish among the Indians and each year some time in March they hold their annual Wild Onion dinner to which the public is invited.

WILD PLUM JELLY

Take wild ripe plums and cook gently in water. Strain in flannel bag and use cup for cup of juice and sugar. Boil until it sheets off the spoon, probably about 8 to 10 minutes. Pour into sterilized glasses.

CRACKLING CORN BREAD

2 cups buttermilk	1 teaspoon soda
1¾ cups corn meal	2 eggs
¼ cup flour	1 teaspoon baking powder

1 cup crackling

Mix as any corn bread and bake.

FRIED WILD HUCKLEBERRIES (A Cherokee Dish)

To fried meat drippings add huckleberries, sprinkle sparingly with sugar and cook until berries are tender.

INDIAN MEAT

1½ pounds round steak cut in pieces 1 inch square. Sprinkle with salt and pepper and roll in flour. Place in an iron skillet with 3 tablespoons of fat, sear on both sides. When brown cover with 2 cups of water and simmer for 1 hour.

CHESTNUT BREAD

Use same recipe as for bean bread substituting uncooked chestnuts. Peel and cut in half about 6 pounds of chestnuts, put into meal and add enough boiling water for dough to hold its shape. Make into round cakes, wrap in corn leaves, drop into boiling water and cook until done.

This group of recipes comes from Mr. and Mrs. William (Bill) Short, Chickasaws, of Davis, Oklahoma. Mr. Short was president during 1953 of the National Congress of American Indians.

BOTA CUPPOSA (Cherokee)

Parched dried corn, beat into flour. Put 2 tablespoons of the flour into a glass, add water and sugar. A traditional drink.

BOFPO (Cherokee)

Parch peanuts and beat them into a fine meal, add 1/3 as much Bota cupposa as peanut meal, mould like butter and slice.

ACORN MUSH (Cherokee)

Beat sweet acorns into a meal, put in a sack and run clear water through them until the strong taste is removed. Use as meal for mush.

WALAKSHI (grape dumplings) (Cherokee)

Wash wild grapes, boil, then strain off juice, sweeten, bring to a boil, add dumplings and cook covered until dumplings are done.

PASHOFA (Chickasaw)

Cook one gallon of corn half done, add ½ gallon pork chopped into small pieces and cook altgether until done. Salt to taste and add a dash of red pepper.

TA-FULLA (Choctaw)

To 1 quart of hominy add 1 gallon of water and ¼ cake of bean ashes. Cook until corn is tender.

BEAN ASH CAKES (Indian soda) (Cherokee)

Put bean hulls in a big pot. Burn until they become ashes. Mix with water, make into small cakes about 3 inches in circumference, and dry in the sun. They are then ready for use.

BANAHA (Cherokee)

Put ½ gallon of hominy in warm water. Soak over night, drain and beat into meal, leaving a part coarse like grits. Take the grits and make into a gruel and pour boiling hot water over the meal. Add cooked beans and bean ashes to make a stiff dough. Make into a roll, wrap in boiled corn shucks and tie in the middle. Boil 4 hours.

PALUSHKA HOWASHKO (sour bread)

Made like banaha except that dough is thinner and beans and bean ashes are omitted. Let the mixture stand until slightly fermented; then bake like corn bread.

SQUAW BREAD

1 pint sweet milk   2 tablespoons baking powder
1 tablespoon shortening   1 teaspoon salt
　　　Flour to make a dough, easily handled.

Knead and roll out to any desired thickness, cut in pieces, cut 2 slits, and cook in kettle of deep fat. Serve with syrup and crisp bacon.

SQUAW BREAD SYRUP

1 quart white corn syrup   1 pound brown sugar

Boil together. Remove from fire, add ½ cup bacon drippings and 1 teaspoon maple flavoring.

From Mr. Lee F. Harkins, Choctaw, former editor of the AMERICAN INDIAN MAGAZINE *comes this comment and recipe.*

"This is a favorite dish among the Osage Indians. With all their wealth, and they are the wealthiest Indian tribe in the world, they love to leave their homes in the villages, load their cars with blankets and camping outfits, go to their farms or some creek, kill a beef, and make their own Stomp-She."

STOMP-SHE

Thoroughly clean one large beef chitterling. Tie one end with a good strong string and stuff into the chitterling one or more fillets of beef, chopped and seasoned with salt and pepper. Tie up other end and boil in water 1½ hours. Serve hot. This can also be baked in a Dutch oven.

Mrs. Lena Finley Barnard, one of the few remaining members of the Piankeshaw Tribe, gave me these traditional recipes from her tribe.

DRIED FISH (Kee-qus-no-swa Po-son-gee)

Dig a pit in the ground, fill with wood fire and let it burn down to red embers, then lay sticks across the pit and place the dressed fish on them. Turn frequently until thoroughly done. Remove from fire, take out all bones and lay in the sun until dry. This meat can be kept indefinitely. Our people stored it away in bags made of buck skins. To prepare this meat it should be moistened and heated. It is very fine creamed.

WAH-WE-NO-KONE-MIN-GUY

Gather green corn when too hard for roasting ears and grate. (The Indians used the jaw of a deer, grating on the teeth.) Place the grated corn in the sun to dry, cook and serve like rice or oatmeal; or it can be used to make bread.

TEAS

Spice wood tea made from broken limbs of spice wood.
Sycamore tea was made from chips of the sycamore tree.
Raspberry tea was made from the raspberry vine.
Sassafras tea was made from the bark of the roots.

MA-CHING-WAH MING-ZAH

Cook burr oak acorns in wood ashes or lye from ashes until the hulls all come off. Wash in several waters and cook with meat.

WATER LILY SEEDS

Gather the seed of large white water lilies, crack the hull of each seed, and then boil in wood ashes or lye from ashes until the hull comes off. Wash several times and cook with game.

PAN-GEE-TAKE MIN-GYP

Parch flour corn, pound, sift out hulls, pour syrup or molasses over the fine siftings and form into balls like popcorn balls.

The coarser siftings are cooked with game.

PO-KEK-KOYL-YOKEE

Gather the roots of large white water lilies, clean, dice, and cook with fish or game. It is very like navy beans.

WAS-LOWE-KEE-PANE-KEE (Wild Potatoes)

Wash clean, tie smaller ones together, and boil with peeling on. When tender remove peeling and eat as domestic potatoes.

The following two recipes were sent to me by Eunice W. Stabler, Wichita, Kansas, Omaha Indian and author of the book "How Beautiful The Land of my Forefathers."

FRIED BREAD

To 3 cups of sifted flour, add 3 teaspoons baking powder, 1 teaspoon salt, 1 heaping teaspoon sugar. Mix well, add 1 cup luke warm water to make up your dough. Add flour, if needed and fry in deep fat much the same as for doughnuts.

STEAMED HUBBARD SQUASH

Peel the squash and cut into small pieces. Place it in a heavy pan which has been greased well, both bottom and sides, add ½ cup cold water and steam for 10 to 15 minutes. At this time add ¼ cup brown sugar and steam 5 minutes longer. Butter may be added, but the Indians did not use it.

Mrs. Alice McCurtain Scott, daughter of Governor Green McCurtain, contributed the following group of recipes.

INDIAN SHUCK BREAD

4 or 5 cups of corn meal   3 cups boiling water

1 teaspoon soda

Scald meal and make into cakes rolled into corn shucks. Drop into rapidly boiling water and boil for 10 minutes.

PREPARING THE TANFULA (Corn)

Most Indians now buy the hominy grits which are bought here in bulk form.

The Indians in preparing their own Tanfula block (usually a log hollowed at the top to form a bowl—a mortar board) and a pestle. For Tonshla Bona they beat the corn until the husk came off, then fanned the husks away.

Some, in making Tanfula, put the corn in the Tanfula block, put in a little wood ashes and a little lukewarm water, then beat the corn to get the kernel out. Then, after fanning the husks off, they washed the corn to get all the lye out of it.

TANFULA (to be eaten fresh) (Tanfula-hominy)

Take any amount of hominy grits or prepared Tanfula (4 cups makes quite a lot). Use enough cold water to cover. Cook over low heat for about 4 hours or longer. Add a pinch of soda in the Tanfula as it starts cooking. When the Tanfula starts getting done it will stick if not stirred often.

SOUR TANFULA

Use any amount of hominy grits or prepared Tanfula or cold water to cover. Cook over a slow fire 4 hours or longer until done. Take a handful of clean wood ashes (some Indians say ashes from a black jack tree are best) put in an iron skillet (the lye in the ashes will eat any other kind of vessel), pour 1 cup boiling water over the ashes, let settle, then strain. Use 2 or 3 tablespoons of the lye water for each gallon of Tanfula. Do not put this lye water in until the Tanfula is nearly done as it will make it mushy if put in too soon. Some Indians used more of this "ash water" in their Tanfula, but Mrs. McCurtain used it sparingly as it is lye. Tanfula made in this way can be put in a crock to sour. This lye will tend to thicken the Tanfula so boil some water and pour over the Tanfula in the crock. It will take perhaps 3 days for this to sour. Tanfula made this way will sour, but it will not rot. If made with soda it cannot be soured, but it will rot.

Mrs. Green McCurtain, wife of the last elected Governor of the Choctaw tribe used this recipe during her lifetime.

TONSHLA BONA

Make a stew of fresh pork back bones or fresh spare ribs or chicken. Cook hominy grits or prepared Tanfula until tender. Add no lye or soda. When the meat and Tanfula are both done combine and cook until the meat has seasoned the Tanfula. Though the Choctaws used no salt the dish should be salted to taste for use to-day.

This recipe comes from the Seminole Reservation in Florida.

PALM (Swamp) CABBAGE

This cabbage grows in swamp areas. When gathering, cut the palm cabbage down near the ground where discoloration begins.

Peel off the outer covering and retain only the core or stem part of the plant. Cut into pieces about 1½ or 2 inches in length and cook like domestic cabbage, using a little salt meat for flavoring. When done it is white and thick. Sometimes eaten with fried fish.

INDIAN CRACKLING CORN PONE (Virginia Algonquian Apan)

Take 2 parts corn meal to one part cracklings, salt to taste. Mix well. Pour boiling water over the mixture until it can be formed with the hands. Form into thin cakes and bake. The Indians baked this in out door ovens or on top of the fire.

The following group of recipes were given me by internationally famous Indian artist, Acee Blue Eagle, and were used by his grandmother.

ABUSKEE

Use roasting ears just before harding. Break a grain to see if kernel is moist. Gather as much corn as you desire to parch. Shell corn in large pan. Sift 1½ gallons dry wood ashes into large iron kettle. Build a fire of medium heat, place kettle over it tilted at a 45 degree angle, pour corn into the ashes and stir continually with wooden paddle until corn is brown. Remove corn and ashes, sift ashes from corn and put back into pot. Continue process until all corn is parched. Pound or grind corn into fine meal. Take 2 heaping teaspoons to one glass of water, sweeten to taste, and you will have the delicious Creek Indian drink called "Abuskee."

SOCK-KO-NIP-KEE (Squirrel and Sofkey Grits)

Prepare one squirrel, place in pot, cover with water and cook until tender. Add 4 cups sofkey grits, cook together until consistency is like hominy. Rice is sometimes used in place of sofkey grits.

SIMI CHUMBO

1 pint sweet milk   3 large tablespoons corn meal

2 tablespoons sugar   3 eggs

Lump of butter   ¼ teaspoon salt

1 cup of hickory nuts—chopped real fine

Bring the milk to a boil, add meal, sugar, butter, and salt and cook slowly until it thickens. Remove from heat, cool, and add the well beaten eggs. Put in a baking pan and bake for 30 minutes in a moderate oven.

CHAD-AH-AH-CHUN-GAH (Blood Pudding)

Thoroughly clean one large hog chitterling, tie one end with a strong string, then stuff into the chitterling the filling prepared for this purpose. Filling: Cook rice in the blood from the hog, season with salt and pepper. When rice is done stuff into the chitterling, tie the other end, and boil for ½ hour. Serve hot. This can also be served cold when it can be sliced if desired.

AH-GEE CHUM-BUH-GEE

1 pound dried fruit
2 cups corn meal, well sifted
2 tablespoons brown sugar

Cook fruit about ½ done in enough water that it will be about 1½ inches over fruit, pour fruit scalding hot over meal, soup and all. If meal is not soft enough to hold its shape with the fruit and fruit soup, add boiling water. Mould into round oblongs and wrap in corn shucks long-wise, tie each end and two or three sections of the middle, drop into boiling water and cook covered until done. These were made especially for Indian children to be used for between meals, like candy or cookies.

Dear heap good fren's I sed it to you
Hope you like it, this cook book too
An' much Injun foods what sed it how to make
Since long ago white mans this country did take.
Now Injun womans forget how to cook
That's sure bad and I think not good
But Mae make Injun Cook Book, now maybe so
You can make Injun food like long ago.
Cook it on *lectic stove, you could
Don't even have to burn it wood.

BY: ACEE BLUE EAGLE

*Electric

THE LEGEND OF CORN

The ancient ones in time of need
Discovered how to use their seed,
The hunters threw aside their bows,
And planted corn in hills and rows.

The blood drenched corn of sacrifice;
The golden song which echoes thrice,
All bow down to the great sun God,
His high priest blesses, smiles and nods.

The Spanish conquerors of old
Took home this seed, instead of gold,
To plant it in the old, old soil,
To bring new life to those who toil.

Today the grain is used for feed,
And mills refine the golden seed;
Over the world the tall corn grows,
The gift of the Indian—the tall green rows.

By Dawn
Great, great granddaughter of Sioux
Chieftain, War Eagle.

ABOUT THE ARTIST

Illustrations for this cook book were done by Acee Blue Eagle, Creek and Pawnee Indian, a great, great grandson of Chief Rolly McIntosh who was leader of his tribe for 31 years.

Acee Blue Eagle has won international fame as an Indian artist. He has done vast research, made hundreds of pencil sketches and notes, to be used in painting authentic records of the various phases peculiar to his people. His work is represented in numerous private collections and museums both in this country and abroad. He has been elected to the Indian "Hall of Fame," Who's Who of Outstanding Indians of the U. S., Who's Who of American Artists, Who's Who of Oklahoma, and International Who's Who.

© Blue Eagle—

Navaho Foods and Cooking Methods
Flora L. Bailey

NAVAHO FOODS AND COOKING METHODS[1] By FLORA L. BAILEY

WITH a few notable exceptions, anthropologists have seldom given the detailed attention to foods and their preparation which, as Dr Audrey Richards has urged,[2] their importance demands. The subject of Navaho foods has been touched upon by several authorities. Actual recipes and directions for preparation have not been given and no survey has been made to determine the extent of individual knowledge of these and other foods. In an attempt at such a survey, twenty-five informants from three areas were questioned about their knowledge and practice of cooking. The data presented and analyzed here are limited to those furnished by women, although information was also secured from four men. Mention will be made of their knowledge later.

The informants were grouped as follows: from the Ramah, New Mexico area, seven women (82, 47, 69, 50, 58, 73, A)[3]; from the Smith Lake-Pinedale area, four women (B, C, D, E); from the Chaco Canyon area, fourteen (F to W inclusive; G, H, V, W, men). Age variation was from fourteen to over sixty years, five being over sixty; six between forty and sixty; nine between twenty and forty; and five under twenty.

The method of procedure was to make friends with the women, watch them cook, and ask as many questions regarding the various foods, their preparation and use, as seemed in keeping with the situation in each case. The first eleven informants, from the Ramah and Smith Lake-Pinedale areas, were not questioned beyond the immediate recipes they were offering. The information given was checked later with the second group of fourteen women in the Chaco Canyon area who consequently did not furnish much new material (only six of the total list of seventy-eight items). Largely because there was considerable anti-white feeling in this area at the time and the women were not inclined to talk freely, all were not questioned on the entire list of foods, although only one was questioned on fewer than twenty-nine and the average number was fifty-nine.

In the Ramah and Smith Lake-Pinedale area the number of foods learned about from individual informants varied from two to forty-six,

---

[1] The writer is under the greatest obligation to Dr Clyde Kluckhohn who gave instruction in field methods and directed this research. She is also deeply grateful to Dr Leland C. Wyman for instruction in recording Navaho, introductions to certain informants, identification of plants, and criticism of the manuscript; and she is indebted to Dr Donald Brand of the University of New Mexico for privileges of its field school.

[2] *Hunger and Work in a Savage Tribe* (London, 1932).

[3] The numbers are those used by Kluckhohn and Tschopik in their publications relating to this group. Informant A is from the neighboring Danoff-Two Wells area.

averaging thirteen. The informants were the more acculturated members of the community except perhaps three of the old women who recalled the use of ancient foods. In the Chaco Canyon area the percentage of affirmative answers given by each woman, indicating her acquaintance with the foods about which she was questioned, ranged from 67.7 to 100, averaging 83.8. This high percentage of affirmative answers made by women in the northern group, more closely adjacent to white culture, to recipes given by the less acculturated women in the other groups indicates that the Navaho tends to retain his food preferences in spite of white influence except in regard to those wild plants and animals which are now very scarce. Without exception, the women who had the most extensive knowledge were members of families where the man was a well known singer in the community. Perhaps their chances of contacting a large number of foods are greater, since it is at a ceremonial that the family serves a quantity of both ancient and modern dishes to the guests.[4] Foods which many of the women professed not to know are those which were evidently in use during the captivity at Fort Sumner and directly after. Such were probably not the preferences of the people at that time but those which were available when all food was scarce. One old man told that while the people were being hunted, and after they were finally set free, they had to eat anything they could lay their hands on or starve.

As other food became available the native foodstuffs and equipment became obsolescent. The women who had not heard of these practices were the younger ones, and those from families where they had no occasion to learn of them through the stories of an older relative. The following are those which were less well known: acorns, wild cherries, dried venison, blister beetle, leeching vegetables, and the use of a native wooden spoon (negative answers, indicating informant disclaimed knowledge of them, seventy-five to one hundred per cent); juniper seeds, squirrel, Orobanchaceae, Amaranthus seeds, juniper tea, storage of seeds, and the storage of roots (fifty to seventy-five per cent negative answers); slim yucca leaves, storage of corn, Ponderosa pine bark, Indian millet, and bear meat (twenty-five to fifty per cent negative answers). Others receiving a few negative replies (less than twenty-five per cent) are: mixed meat decoction, jack rabbit stew, fruit of the prickly pear cactus, Tradescantia, thin corn griddle cakes, Navaho tea, native salt, seeds of Sporobolus, Descurania, and Chenopodium, locusts, and the use of corn-stirring sticks. It will be seen that even though there were a large number of items unfamiliar to some women,

---

[4] Washington Matthews has noted this in *The Night Chant, A Navaho Ceremony* (Memoirs, American Museum of Natural History, Vol. 6, 1902).

almost half of these were unknown to only a few. Of the last group, the corn foods, Navaho tea, locusts, and corn-stirring sticks were things unknown to less than ten per cent of the women.

Matthews, in the Night Chant,[5] listed twenty-one ancient foods served as part of the ceremonial procedure during the vigil of the fourth night. Of these, eleven were mentioned by my informants. In addition, others mentioned by Matthews and also known to my informants were squashes, yucca, other wild fruits, wheaten cakes, mutton, and dried peaches. In the Chaco Canyon area nearly all the women knew these foods, and in the Ramah area about half of the women mentioned all of them even though not specifically questioned. Only three were mentioned by the Smith Lake-Pinedale group. The Franciscan Fathers[6] list about one hundred and twenty foods of which thirty-six were mentioned by my informants. These were twelve (of thirty-three) corn foods (nine also in Matthews' list); thirteen (of forty) wild plants, seeds, fruits or berries; eleven (of thirty-eight) meats or ways of preparing meat. Here again the Chaco Canyon women rated high in their knowledge, and the Ramah ones about the same as in their knowledge of ancient foods. Hill[7] mentions fourteen foods of which seven were known to my informants. Of the seventy-eight items given in this paper forty have not been found mentioned in the literature on the subject.

Although the Franciscan Fathers mentioned the stone griddle as a common utensil, its use seems to have disappeared in the areas studied except for making paper bread. They also say that sticks in uneven numbers (from one to eleven) are always used together for stirring corn dishes, the smaller numbers being preferred. The old women whom I questioned said that any number, from one up, may be used but that four is the preferred number. While goat meat is at present a common part of the Navaho diet, it is not given in the Franciscan's list.

Of the foods listed, certain ones seem to be preferred for every day use.

[5] Matthews, *op. cit.* paragraphs 218 to 233 inclusive and page 107. Indicated in my list at the end of this paper by the letter M.

[6] Franciscan Fathers, *An Ethnologic Dictionary of the Navaho Language* (Saint Michaels, Arizona, 1910). Indicated in my list at the end of this paper by the letter F.

[7] W. W. Hill, *Agricultural and Hunting Methods of the Navaho Indians* (Yale University Publications in Anthropology, No. 18, 1938).

Other writers who have furnished material on Navaho foods are Francis Elmore, *Food Animals of the Navaho* (El Palacio, Vol. 44, nos. 22–24, June 1–15, 1938), E. F. Castetter, *Uncultivated Native Plants used as sources of food* (Albuquerque, 1935; *passim.*) and Gladys A. Reichard, *Social Life of the Navajo Indians* (Columbia University Contributions to Anthropology Vol. VII, Columbia University Press, New York City, 1928).

For example, of the seventeen kinds of bread, only three or four are commonly made, the tortillas, the fried and baked bread (all of wheat flour), and the green corn bread in the summer time. The corn breads are served mainly on ceremonial occasions although they may be more generally in use during the winter than in summer. There is little difference to be observed between the food used in the three areas in question. The daily diet of mutton or goat meat, coffee, wheat flour bread, and potatoes, with an occasional addition of canned or fresh fruit and vegetables is about the same in all homes. Of course the financial status of the family at the moment will influence greatly the variety, especially of store foods.

In watching several women prepare the same article at different times a certain amount of variation was observed. This was due mainly to availability of material, *i.e.* water used if milk was not handy, and vegetable fat used in preference to tallow if the women could afford it; and to some extent it varied between women who had attended school and received lessons in cooking and those who had less contact with white culture. The foods which showed no variation were the corn foods prepared with or without juniper ashes. This may have been because they are used ceremonially hence their preparation is prescribed.

COOKING EQUIPMENT AND UTENSILS

Most of the hogans observed had at least two arrangements for cooking, a stove indoors, and a fire pit outdoors. The stove is used in bad weather, or in winter, while the outdoor fire is used for most of the summer cooking. Two types of stoves were seen. One was a small, American, wood-burning stove with an oven for baking. The pipe extended through the open smoke hole in the hogan roof, or through the loose branches of the shade. The other type was of home construction, made of material from the left-overs at the trading post. It was a cylindrical, tapering arrangement of old wash tubs or oil drums, the bottoms removed, cemented together with adobe and supported on stones about a foot high. It protruded through the smoke hole. A small fire is built under it and cooking pots set around it, poked under the edge of the "stove." Often this type is set up in the summer shade as well as in the hogan. Both types are easily removed if the floor space is needed for other purposes. Sometimes there is no stove in the hogan, simply the older method of building a fire on the floor under the smoke hole.

Firewood (čiž) is almost without exception juniper unless unavailable. In that case pinyon may be used, if this also is unavailable, chamiso. Dry juniper wood (diłkiz) makes a fine fire, has a pleasant odor, gives a clear smoke and does not blacken the pans. Pinyon makes a pitchy smoke and ruins the pots. Chamiso makes a vile odor and does not hold the heat. Usually a Navaho fire is small and compact, being started with chips and twigs, and a few larger sticks added as needed. No woman builds such a large fire that she can't get close to it when necessary.

The Spanish oven, of the beehive shape seen in pueblos, is sometimes found outside a hogan and has probably been built for use during a ceremonial. One woman stated that they are only used to cook for big crowds, such as those at Enemy Way, as they are too much trouble generally.

Additional cooking equipment usually includes storage space for dishes and food. This ranges from improvised shelves of orange crates to the most modern kitchen cabinets. There may also be a table, sometimes covered with bright oilcloth, in the more sophisticated hogans. These kitchen furnishings invariably occupy the north side of the hogan or shade, rather nearer the door than the back of the room.

Cooking utensils proper include the following: pottery jars, either Pueblo or Navaho, for cooking and serving; sometimes a basket for serving certain foods; store dishes in tin and crockery ware; knives, spoons, and forks; and one or two cast iron frying pans or Dutch ovens on three legs. Two indispensable items are the grass brooms, or brushes (bé·ʔéžó·ʔ), and the corn-stirring sticks (ʔé·désci·n), made of chamiso (dówóži·)—Atriplex canescens (Pursh) Nutt. In one hogan seven brushes were counted, some new, some nearly worn away. They are used for hair brushes also, one end for cooking, the other for the hair. They are about a foot long and two inches in diameter at the stubby end, fanning out at the other. The stirring sticks, used for corn dishes only, are not thrown away but used over and over. In use they are held in the right hand like a pencil, fingers turned down and pointing toward the body, the pressure being against the last three fingers while stirring. After use they are leaned against the edge of the pan on the ground.

Three other utensils, now no longer in favor, were used in the old days: wooden spoons made from juniper warts (gad bise·s) and shaped with a stone knife, pottery spoons of various sizes, and spoons made from shaped gourds. Now commercial forks, knives, and spoons are used for both cooking and eating, although the preferred method is to use the more convenient fingers.

One arrangement for holding a hot dish while stirring was a strip of metal, about eighteen inches long and two inches wide, held in the left hand, one end placed against the rim of the hot container, and the other end resting on the ground, braced under the left knee while the right hand stirred the contents.

The metal griddle (cétʼeˑs) for baking griddle cakes is usually a sheet of metal about twenty inches square, supported over the fire by stones or empty evaporated milk cans. This and the coffee pot are the household's most frequently used articles.

Most families still possess the stone equipment, metate (čaˑšžéˑ?) or (cébenálžoˑh) and mano (čaˑšžíní), for grinding wheat, corn, and seeds. One woman, over sixty, owns a very old stone for grinding grass and flower seeds (γʷoˑsċe? beˑḱá), size about four by three inches. Held in the right hand the grinding motion is circular rather than pulling as in grinding corn.

CUSTOMARY PRACTICES IN FOOD PREPARATION

Method of grinding corn: The corn, previously dried, is first roasted for about five minutes in a frying pan over the coals, constantly stirring to prevent burning. Then it is laid on a sheepskin, spread hide up on the ground, to cool. A metate is placed on the middle of the skin and the corn is ground three times, using a grass brush for sweeping the meal. The meal is stored in small sugar or flour sacks.

Method of grinding wheat: Wheat is dried in the sun on a canvas and ground as is corn, but four times instead of three, for it is harder to grind (82) and should make a finer flour.

Method of grinding native salt: Chunks of grayish salt are ground as is corn, but using the hand to sweep the stone, and stored in cloth sacks. One woman worked with a baby in her lap, the child learning the movement by placing her hands between her sister's on the mano and later imitating it.

Methods of measuring: Women who have attended school, or are acculturated, measure flour, milk, and the like by cups. The older and more usual method is by handfuls. Frequently the former was used only when an observer was recording the recipe. The consistency of the dough is a common guide in adding liquids. Baking powder and salt are measured by scooping some into the cupped, four fingers of the right hand, indicating the amount by an imaginary line drawn with the thumb across either the first or second joints. They seem to know by long practice what proportions should be used.

Method of Purifying Water: Water, from the storage barrels, is strained through a piece of flour sacking fastened over a wire loop on a handle. The strained water has about the same color as before, but the women seem satisfied that it is cleaner.

Method of Combining Shortening and Other Ingredients in Bread: Shortening is added to the liquid, rather than the dry ingredients of the recipe, and squeezed until it floats in small lumps. The flour is then added slowly and thoroughly mixed, kneading with the hands. Dough mixed this way is seldom lumpy, strange to say, but "it wouldn't matter anyway for it always tastes all right" (82).

Method of Hauling Water: Water is scarce although government wells have made it more accessible in recent years. It is drawn by rope and bucket, emptied into barrels, washtubs, or other large containers covered with gunny sacking, and hauled by wagon to its customary place. Heavy barrels are more easily handled by backing the wagon into a shallow pit which brings it on a level with the ground. Hauling water and cutting firewood are men's duties but are undertaken by women when necessary.

Cleanliness: Although Navaho standards of cleanliness are not those of a New England housewife, one gets the impression that the women take a certain pride in keeping the hogan neat and clean, sweeping the ground around the cooking fire with a twig broom, washing the hands frequently, serving food graciously and tastefully, especially when guests are present, and washing the dishes in hot water at least part of the time. Sometimes they overlook the fact that the dish towel is a filthy rag, that a hair has fallen in the bread batter, that someone may have washed his hands in the drinking water, or that flies are swarming on the food. 82 stated that a corn noodle which has fallen on the floor must never be picked up and used, not indicating whether this was because of cleanliness or superstition. Meat freshly butchered is cleaned, cut in pieces, and hung in the shade over wires to keep it away from dogs and dirt. It is usually cooked thoroughly and eaten immediately, any surplus being given to the relatives and friends.

Cooperation in Cooking: The women of the household work together to prepare the meals, cheerfully and congenially, but anyone present may be drafted to help, even the men. Some men, however, will only cook if the women are sick, or there is no one else to do it. On two occasions men were observed to offer help, watching food lest it burn, when the woman was busy elsewhere. One man, from Ramah (24), was several times observed making bread when his wife was actually present. Children, both boys and girls, are expected to help by tending the fire, running errands, and washing dishes. One small boy was seen to take sole charge of watching the broiling meat, and at the same time he fried cucumbers very skillfully. Some children are taught to cook, others learn by imitation. 47 taught her daughters to cook at five, and weave at ten years of age, although she wasn't taught by her mother. 82 says children have to be taught today because they don't mind their parents. In the old days of strict obedience they learned by imitation. Male informants (G, H) learned to cook by watching, and think it quite customary for men to do so.

Food Preferences and Feeding Methods: Certain food prejudices are widespread. Many will not eat eggs because it will make them have babies all the time, one a year, nor fish and bacon because they are not clean (82). Chickens are not eaten either, yet they are seen frequently around the hogan; perhaps they make good pets. Most of the Ramah group who keep chickens do eat eggs. They have kept chickens only about ten years.

Food preferences are individual. One woman likes corn foods, goat and sheep head, intestines, blood sausage, and sprouted wheat cake, but will not eat dried squash or yucca fruit. Her five children include in their dislikes butter, intestines, milk, candy, jam, sandwich spread, sardines, and canned meat. One girl had ceremonial restrictions placed on fish, and sheep entrails, preventing her from eating them. The first occurred because she became ill, due to her mother having seen a bloated fish while carrying her, but was cured by a ceremonial in which a fish image was made, placing, therefore, a ban on it.

In another family the father has a great fondness for chili peppers and peanut butter, while his two-year-old daughter loves canned meat above all else. Two men (G, H) sheepishly admit to a liking for locusts, baked in the coals, as do three women also (P, Q, R). The often retold story of the dislike of coffee by the old people due to the early misuse of the berries caused amusement whenever mentioned. Leeching of vegetables seems unknown to the women, although they express a preference for vegetables served without the juices as they are more palatable, especially wild potatoes and wild spinach.

Babies are nursed at the breast for several months, after which some women put them on a bottle. If a mother has no milk another woman may furnish it[8] or the baby may be put directly on a bottle of canned milk and warm water. After approximately eight months the child is fed whatever the rest of the family eats, but may still be nursed intermittently for three years. Some women, having been to school, add orange juice and canned baby food to the diet, giving no solid food for one year.

During pregnancy a woman eats carefully. 82 says she eats the same food but in smaller quantities, having lost her appetite. 73 believes fattening foods, especially milk, should be avoided as they make the baby fat. After the child is born the mother is fed corn meal mush to give her strength, and juniper tea to bring the placenta (73), (other herb decoctions are also used). Restrictions are placed on the mother for several days against meat, potatoes, beans, and bread containing either salt or baking powder. This prevents recurrence of the pains and aids in healing the baby's cord (73).

---

[8] *Cf.* Walter Dyk, *Son of Old Man Hat* (Harcourt, Brace, and Co. New York 1938) p. 3.

Blue corn mush or gruel will bring about unaided the recovery of an invalid.

Store foods form an important element in the diet. Flour, sugar, coffee, and potatoes are staples, with canned meat, fruit, and vegetables a luxury. Canned peaches and tomatoes are very popular, as are melons in season, although the latter are sometimes raised by the family and are not primarily store products. Sometimes an acculturated family includes crackerjack and sweets with the ancient corn cake given away at the girls puberty ceremony.

ETIQUETTE AND EATING CUSTOMS

The manner of serving guests varies with individual families. Some expect white guests to eat with the family; some serve them first, setting a special "table" on a blanket on the floor and providing adequate crockery and utensils; some never ask a white guest to have food. Generally the guests and the men are served first, the women and children eating after the others have finished. At ceremonials food is offered graciously whenever guests approach the cook-shade.

82 remarked that most people just eat bread and coffee unless there are guests, then they must have something more from the store, perhaps potatoes and fruit. Women herding sheep alone don't care how they cook because they are in a hurry, they just eat quickly (F).

It is improper for a woman to stand while cooking. She sits on the ground if outdoors, or on a bench if using a stove in the hogan. The older women say it is impolite for either a man or woman to remain standing in the hogan, though a man may occasionally do so. However, women were observed standing by an outdoor fire to tend food if other things needed attention at the same time. They bend from the waist, knees straight, and hold their full skirts back from the flames with one hand.

Members of a burial party are required to eat from separate dishes for the four days of mourning, after which time the dishes can be again used by the rest of the family.

FOLK BELIEFS AND PRACTICES CONCERNING FOODS

Care must be taken in gathering the fruit of the prickly pear cactus (hᵂoš dižo·li·) Opuntia sp. It is the same thing as (žé·nayogísi·) which means "twists the heart" (P). A hair must be plucked from the gatherer's head and offered the plant so that it will yield its fruit without twisting his heart. Such precautions need be taken with no other plant.

A kitten caught stealing food should have its ears pierced and threaded with small bead earrings. This prevents further stealing (47).

Left-handedness in women seems undesirable. F wonders if it is "right" to cook left-handed. It is awkward, she says, unless you do so naturally, then it may not be so bad. Sometimes men do not like to marry a left-handed woman since she looks queer, being different.

A melon is never cut by piercing with the point of a knife but is cut "around."

Eating burned foods may bring drastic results. Burned bread will give you "baked blood" and might kill you. Any burned article would react the same way, hurt your throat and make the blood come out your mouth (P, Q, R, S). You can dispose of the food by feeding it to the animals as it can not hurt them. Corn meal sprinkled over the kinalda cake while a prayer is said will prevent it burning. This is the only cake so treated (P, Q, R, S).

Corn dumplings must always be flattened in shape in the summer. If made into balls, as in winter, the hail will come, as large as the dumplings, and ruin the crops (82, 47, I). 73 says corn noodles should never be made in the summer.

A boy is never allowed to eat Blue Corn Mush from the stirring sticks (although girls may do so) as it will cause his hand to tremble while taking aim in hunting (47). This restriction is now obsolescent (I).

NAVAHO RECIPES[9]

BREADS AND CAKES

Breads Made of Corn Flour

no·gá·zá—*Thin Corn Griddle Cakes* (M, F).

Mix four or five cups of corn flour with a little baking powder and enough goat's milk and hot water (or all milk) to make a thick batter. Cook on a greased, metal sheet in cakes about six inches in diameter, turning to cook both sides about three minutes each. I uses only hot water and both baking powder and cedar ashes. M called this dish ʔabeʔ be·ne·zmosí.

nadą́·ʔ ná nes ka·dí—*Shaped Corn Griddle Cakes* (M, F).

Mix one cup juniper ashes with water and strain through a grass brush into basin of corn flour, using about three and one-half cups of the liquid. Add one-half cup clear water to this greenish dough and knead until thick. Shape with moist hands into round cakes less than an inch thick and four inches in diameter. Bake on a dry griddle, rubbing it with a cloth between bakings, and moisten cakes on both sides when done.

---

[9] Descriptive terms are used for foods rather than an accurate translation of Navaho names.

kíne·š bíži—*Corn Dumplings* (M, F).

Make a dough of corn flour, juniper ashes, and boiling water (to prevent breaking while cooking—82). I mixes cold water with the flour before adding the hot. Shape into patties by rotating bits of dough in a pan, flatten if desired, and drop in a pail of boiling water to cook one hour. One woman was seen rolling dumplings by hand, two at a time, into flat, circular cakes two inches by one-half inch thick, and boiling only fifteen minutes. A gruel may be made of the cooking water by adding a little dough, thinned with water. Shaped Corn Griddle Cakes can be made from the same dough.

nadą́· ʔłe·sʔá·ń[10]—*Corn Bread Baked in Ashes* (M, F).

Strain about one cup hot water mixed with juniper ashes through a grass brush into two cups blue corn flour, adding the liquid gradually and kneading with the hands to form a heavy dough. Shape into flat, oblong cakes one inch by one-half inch by five inches. Bake in the ashes for one hour. When done they will sound hollow if tapped with a stick. Brush off the ashes and wash to remove final traces before serving.

tá na·š gi·ž—*Blue Corn Mush* (M, F).

Add three-fourths cup strained cedar ashes and water to three or four cups water and boil briskly. Add four large handfuls blue corn flour and boil for thirty minutes, stirring frequently with corn-stirring sticks. Remove from fire and stir until very thick. Serve with yucca preserves in winter.

céʔesťéi·—*Paper Bread* (M, F).

A thin, corn meal batter is spread with the level palm in one stroke on a hot griddle. It is very hard to make (F).

ncidogoʔi—*Green Corn Bread* (M, F, H).

Scrape the kernels from three dozen ears of green corn and grind either on a metate or through a meat chopper. Make small packages of the mush by wrapping in two green corn husks, the first folded over and laid face down on the second. Place these boat-like packages in a hollow in the coals, cover with freshly picked squash leaves, slightly moist dirt, and hot coals. Build a quick fire over the coals and bake one hour. Eat at once, or let harden and dry in the sun, removing outer husk after first day. Store and use in winter, broken in pieces and boiled with meat or steamed and served with salt. Called in this form łe·sʔá·ńbeską (82). Sometimes baked in a Spanish oven (P), salt added (O), made daily in the autumn (I).

---

[10] Shaped Corn Griddle Cakes and Green Corn Bread may also be called by this name.

Breads Made of both Corn and Wheat Flour

ʔaˑlkaˑn—*Kinalda Cake* (M, F).

This is used in the girls puberty ceremony. Proportions given here are for a sample cake made by 58 for the author. To one-half pail boiling water add six handfuls white corn flour. Stir with corn-stirring sticks, then add one cup sprouted wheat flour (dínésą̨—green wheat, placed in a sack under ground to sprout, then dried and ground on a metate) and continue stirring. Remove mush from fire and cool ten or fifteen minutes. Rub and squeeze between the palms, as if washing the hands, until all the lumps are removed (about thirty minutes). Moisten dry corn husks and tear down the ends one-half inch in five or six places. Make a cross of husks (two on the bottom and one on top) pinning firmly with a short piece of grass broom straw. Join the tips of the east and south arms of the cross with two more husks. Similarly close the other three quadrants, working sunwise (58). Add other husks thus making a mat. Rake coals out of a pit (eighteen by six inches) in which a fire burned for about four hours, brush with juniper branches and place the corn husk mat on the bottom. Lay more husks around the sides, tucking these under the mat. Pour the mush into the pit and smoothe. Sprinkle cornmeal on the surface from east to west, south to north, and around sunwise. Meal is always sprinkled on this kind of a cake "to make it holy," even a sample one (82). Cover with corn husks, then a layer of dirt, then the hot coals. Build a fire on top and bake three or four hours. Remove dirt and ashes using juniper branch and grass broom. The first piece should be cut from the center and divided into four parts, although in this instance it was cut from the northwest corner. When hot the cake is quite mushy but it hardens when cold. When made for the puberty ceremony there must be at least four big pieces, one for the singer and the others for those who helped sing (58).

łeˑhiˑlžoˑž—*Baked White Corn Tamales* (M, F)

Use same dough as for Kinalda Cake adding sugar, or masticated corn, uncommon now, for sweetening (F, 50). Wrap in corn husks as follows: lay out two husks end to end, butts overlapping by four inches, fold sides over the dough, then the ends, and tie in three places, crosswise, with corn husk strips. Bake in hot coals.

daʔanžiló·ʔi—*Boiled White Corn Tamales.*

Add boiling water to white corn flour and stir with corn-stirring sticks to make a thick paste. Add flour and water alternately, stirring constantly, then one cup sprouted wheat flour. Knead by squeezing and turning until heavy dough is formed. Lay moistened corn husks in pairs, the tip of the upper husk overlapping the butt of the lower, and pointing the same way. Place mush in the center, add a third husk for the top, roll the sides of lower husks over the top, tie at each end and in the center with strips of husk, and tie on a husk handle, lengthwise. Place in boiling water and cook one-half hour. Serve hot or cold. They are sweeter and harder if allowed to cool (82).

ʔabeʔbeˑneˑẓmosí or kánheˑzką̨[11]—*Milk Blue Corn Griddle Cakes.*

Place two cups milk in a pan, adding one teaspoon baking powder and one-fourth teaspoon salt. Stir in two handfuls blue corn flour and one-half cup wheat flour, to keep the cakes from cracking. Pour the thin batter on a greased griddle and bake three minutes on each side.

X̌oh nadą̨ˑʔłeˑsʔáˑń—*Green Corn and Wheat Cake.*

New wheat, four inches high, is cut and ground then mixed with corn and made into cakes (not made in summer as they spoil).

Breads Made of Wheat Flour

dadíniˑlɣaž—*Fried Bread.*

Combine two cups flour, one-half teaspoon salt, and one teaspoon baking powder. Add one tablespoon vegetable shortening to about one-half cup water which has been poured into a hole in the dry ingredients. Knead and squeeze the fat into the water, then into the flour, using the hands and working it into a springy dough. Taking a piece of dough the size of a tennis ball, pull and slap it back and forth between the knuckles until it forms a flat cake about ten inches in diameter and one-half inch thick. Fry in deep fat three minutes on each side, turning and removing with a fork. It will puff up making a brown, crisp bread about an inch thick. Sometimes a hole is made in the center before frying, for the grease to come through (82).

nánes kaˑdí—*Wheat Tortillas* (H).

Use same dough as for fried bread, but shape by first rolling long coils of the dough, as if for pottery, and then flatten into large cakes with a wooden rolling pin on a low table, four inches high. Bake on a griddle for fifteen minutes, turning once or twice. Never made with a hole in the center (82).

kisânîˑmaza or kisânîˑ bi báˑh—*Baked Wheat Bread.*

---

[11] 82 said that these are wheat flour cakes made the same as corn but one-half teaspoon salt added.

Shape the dough used for fried bread into balls and place in greased muffin tins, or pat into flat ovals four inches long and lay on a baking sheet. Bake in Spanish or American oven turning when half done.

bá·h—*Yeast Bread.*

A brownish loaf resembling soda bread, baked either in a Dutch oven over coals or in a Spanish oven if quantities are being made (F). No recipe obtained.

ʔine·š bíži ćosí·—*Wheat Noodle for Soup* (H).

Combine one cup flour, pinch of salt, one-third cup fat, and enough water to make a thick dough. Knead thoroughly, roll pencil sized coils between the palms, break into two inch lengths, and drop in boiling water for one-half hour. Make a soup by adding meat, or one tablespoon fat, and red pepper to season (82).

MEATS

Domesticated Animals

dibé bici·n bi bé·ž—*Boiled Mutton* (F).

Cut meat from the bones, break up the bones, add salt and boil, well covered with water, until done. Green corn may be added if desired.

ʔabé·ž—*Boiled Sheep or Goat Entrails* (F).

Heart, liver, and lungs, boiled for about three hours.

ʔałťaʔná·bé·ž—*Mixed decoction.*[12]

Sheep entrails boiled together in a pottery jar with roots and seeds of watermelon, roots and seeds of squash, and sweet corn.

dibé bici·n sikaʔasťé—*Broiled Mutton* (F).

Meat is broiled slowly, turning frequently, on a grate over the coals. Salt is added.

ł̣iži bici·n sitʼé—*Baked Goat's Meat.*

Meat is baked in a shallow pan in an oven, turning occasionally, for one and one-half hours.

ʔaʔći·ʔi sitʼé—*Baked Sheep or Goat's Head* (F).

Singe the hair from the head and place it, together with the feet, in a hole in which a fire has burned for an hour. Cover with coals, build a fire on top and bake for about four hours. When done the ashes are removed and the tongue, brains, eyes, and jaw muscles eaten. The head can be baked in an oven if desired.

---

[12] Kluckhohn and Wyman (in preparation) will give more complete details.

dił—*Blood Sausage* (F).

Cut a goat or sheep's throat and catch the blood in a pan. Let stand one-half hour, then squeeze and stir with the hands, discarding the lumpy parts. Add two and one-half cups diced intestines, and other meat. Mix and place in sheep's stomach, tying the holes, or tying in small bundles like sausages. Boil for two hours. It will keep a day and one-half only (82).

ʔałḱiń ʔiˑlgiž—*Dried Mutton* (F).

Cut meat in thin slices, salt, and hang over wires to dry. May be stored and later served boiled, or as a soup. Venison, unlike mutton, must be pounded and soaked in hot water before eating (50). Beef, pounded and dried, is called ʔáčǫʔ (L).

Wild Animals

gah coh bi béˑž—*Jack Rabbit Stew* (F).

Dress the rabbit and boil it with corn flour and salt. This was used by the old people (82). Meat may also be fried (P, Q, R, S).

λoziłgai—*Squirrel* (H).

The gray, long-tailed squirrel was formerly fried, or cleaned and baked in coals with the hair on. It is no longer used (50, F, G, H, P, Q, R, S).

łeʔécoh—*Pack Rat* (F).

Clean, without removing the hair, salt the meat, and bake in coals. Some say it is still used for food (I, 50), others that it is not (F, G, H). Prairie dog (λǫˑ) is prepared in the same manner, or the hair may be singed off before baking in a hole in the ground.

šaš—*Bear* (F).

Some people avoid eating this meat believing that it is not good for you (G, H, M, P, Q, R, S) and will make you too "mean." 82 and 50 say that a small piece will protect you if you don't eat too much. It was more often eaten long ago when food was scarce.

γʷoneˑščíˑdi—*Locusts*.

Remove legs, wings, and head of insect. Brown the rest in the ashes and eat. It tastes like peanuts (P). Used to be eaten in the old days but now mostly by children. Used as medicine to cure stomach ache and prevent measles (M), prevent smallpox or other contagious diseases (50), and to cure sore throat by administering in a cold infusion both internally and externally together with dried Tradescantia sp., céʔéžíˑh—Artemisia Wrightii Gray, and tôi káˑł—Artemisia frigida Willd. Administer twice with an interval of several hours (P).

diẓéʔyołyéˑhiˑ—*Megetra vittata* (LcConte). Blister Beetle.

The only informant mentioning the blister beetle said the people used it for food in the old days. She herself never ate any (50).

CULTIVATED VEGETABLES

nómazí coh—*White Potatoes.*

Prepared in many ways: fried in vegetable fat, adding water when soft to make a mush (C), fried with onions and salt (D), boiled with goat's meat or mutton (E), fried without onions (82, 73), or baked in a Dutch or American oven (M).

nadą́ˑʔ—*Green Corn* (F, H).

Prepared in many ways: as bread (see Breads); cut from cob and boiled with goat's milk sometimes adding the fruit of ná bị·h—Conioselinum scopulorum (Gray) C. & R. (82), though I and O denied this; boiled with meat (haníˑgai), sometimes with diced squashes; boiled on the cob; fried (M); and roasted, either in a pit (łeˑšibéˑž) or in an oven. The roasting pit is made in the ground, five and one half feet deep and twenty inches diameter at the top, but hollowed out below so it is larger there. A fire is kept going in it all day, then removed, and the corn (two wagon loads) put in, covered with corn leaves and dirt, and roasted all night (A). Remove husks and eat at once, or dry for winter when it can be boiled in water, or ground and eaten in coffee (47).

naγízí—*Squash* (F).

Diced, boiled in water, and served salted (ši béˑž). Peeled, cut in thin strips and fried in mutton fat (sa naˑsciˑd). Quartered and baked in the oven or over an open fire (naγíz siťéʔ), or baked in the ashes. Dried for the winter it may be either náhinesťą́ˑz—big squashes "cut around" in strips (P), or little squashes cut in long strips (šanilťáˑz) (P, 50). Takes three or four days to dry as it must be taken in if it rains. After drying it is scorched briefly on the coals, then boiled as a soup adding corn flour (82).

Cucumbers.

On one occasion a woman was observed preparing cucumbers from the store by dicing and frying in deep fat in a Dutch oven. She said she had never tried cooking them before but thought she might like them that way.

WILD PLANTS

nómazí yáží—*Solanum Jamesii* Torr. (F)

Boiled unpeeled and mashed in the hands (as if kneading dough); fried, fresh, in tallow (F); cut into pieces and dried for the winter. After drying they may be boiled into a kind of pudding (50), or ground into flour which is made into griddle cakes (with water) (I), or mixed with goat's milk to make a porridge (A). To obviate the unpleasant, sour taste (82), or to prevent poisoning (M), a bit of rhyolite tuff (ʌeˑš) mixed with water is added in cooking wild potatoes although 82 said her children eat them raw without becoming sick.

nahóˑyai—*a root resembling sweet potato* (unidentified). (F).

Root is boiled and eaten like a potato (50), principally used during the stay at Fort Sumner (F). Dried, then soaked in water and pounded on a stone it is now used to make a suds, which causes hair washed in it to grow very long. The root of čašdéˑ ži· (*Phellopterus bulbosus* (A. Nels.) (C. & R.) is also eaten, being chewed and eaten raw, or dried and used as flour (B, C).

ʌ'oh čin—*Allium cernum Roth., var. neomexicanum* (Rydb.) Mach.

Wild onions eaten raw (82); used in soups and gravies (I); dried for the winter (I).

ki·lcini·—*probably Tradescantia spp.*

ki·lcini·lčí—*Calochortus Gunnisonii* Wats

The entire plant is boiled and eaten like spinach (50), or baked in the coals (I, P, Q, R, S), being only used in the spring.

ʌ'oh deˑs k̓idi·?—*Amaranthus retroflexus L.*

After boiling the leaves about an hour add one-half cup tallow and some salt (82). May be used like squash blossoms for flavoring; now obsolescent (I).

ɫe·do·leˑz—*various species of Orobanchaceae.*

"Grows under a bush and looks like asparagas" (82). Baked in the ashes, obsolete (82); dried, ground, and rubbed on sores as a medicine (M).

cá?ászi?čóˑz—*Yucca glauca* Nutt.

The leaves of the slim yucca are tied in bundles, boiled, and eaten with salt (50). Obsolete.

ńdíščí·? biťáťahí—*bark of Pinus ponderosa* Laws.

In the summer the inner bark is eaten with salt (A). Obsolete (F). Obsolescent except in forested parts of the reservation (I). P, Q, R, and S said another tree (de·sbái) is similarly used.

WILD SEEDS

ʌ'oh čóˑzí—*Sporobolus cryptandrus* (Torr.) Gray. (F).

Ground and cooked before eating (F). Ground, mixed with milk and served as beverage.

X'oh de·—*various species of Chenopodium* (probably *C. leptophyllum* (Moq.) Nutt. or *C. Fremontii* Wats.) (M, F).

The seeds are threshed by heaping the plants on a sheepskin and beating them with a stick. Prepared like corn (M); ground and made into bread (82); or prepared in any of the following ways (50): baked as a cake in a pit oven in the ground, baked as a griddle cake (X'oh de· ɫe·sʔá·ń), made into a mush, or used as flavoring in corn cakes.

ʔósceʔ or X'osce—*Descurainia Sophia* (L.) Webb. (F).

Seeds were formerly gathered by patting the blossoms with a pottery ladle over a pottery jar (A), or in a basket. Seeds rubbed in the hands to free them from husks, ground on a stone and served by stirring in cold water as a beverage, by making into bread, or by eating the mashed pulp and drinking the juice.

ńdeXídi—*Oryzopsis hymenoides* (Roem. and Schult.) Ricker.

A sweet grass, scarce today therefore obsolescent (A). Prepared by burning to ashes, then grinding and adding the powder to goat's milk; or by making into bread.

na·zka·di·—*various species of Amaranthus* (probably *A. blitoides* Wats.).

Seeds are threshed by the method described for *Chenopodium* and similarly prepared; ground and kneaded into dough with water then shaped in long loaves and baked in the ashes.[13] This bread (na·zká·d ɫe·sʔá·ń) is always made in this shape (F).

diɫtá·lí or gad biná·ʔ—juniper fruit.

These are sweet like sugar (50) and were ground and eaten in mush (obsolete). P said that dika·s (unidentified) was also "sweet like sugar," but cultivated and used for candy.

ne·ščí·ʔ—*seeds of Pinus edulis* Engelm. (F).

Roast the pinyon nuts in a frying pan until they crack. Grind carefully to break shells, and winnow in a pan. Mix with roasted dried corn and eat thus; or grind fine and mold into a small cake on the metate, dry in the sun, and keep for winter (82). "Peanut Butter" may be made by grinding the nuts (P, Q, R, S).

čéčil biná·ʔ—*acorns* (F).

Eaten when ripe (A). Formerly ground into a mush and eaten, but never roasted (A).

---

[13] Mr Tschopik has noted the use of the following edible seeds for bread on the part of the people in the Ramah area: náčíšžáni—Chenopodium incanum (Wats.) Heller., X'oh de hʷoši—Amaranthus retroflexus L., X'oh de·nX'izi—Atriplex rosea L., and ɫe·aze—Eriogonum alatum Torr. (Identification of plants by Dr Leland C. Wyman.)

BERRIES AND FRUITS

či·lčin—*Rhus canadensis* Marsh., *var. trilobata* (Nutt.) Gray. (F).

Bark is eaten with salt (50). Berries are dried, ground, and mixed with
sugar and water like jam (F, I) though in the old days no sugar was used.
Bark and berries may both be ground to form a jelly (P, Q, R, S).

kínžíłʔa·hí—*Ribes inebrians* Lindl. (F).

Wild currants are generally eaten without specific preparation.

ha·šče·ʔdą́·ʔ—*Lycium Torreyi* Gray.

Fresh berries are ground on a stone, sugar added, and served as mush,
sometimes adding rhyolite tuff to sweeten them (M, P, Q, R, S). 47 never
heard of eating berries and meat together, or adding them with nuts to corn
foods. Dried berries are boiled for one-half hour, ground, and eaten with
wild potatoes (A), or made into a mush with water (82).

ndoλohí—*fruit of Yucca glauca* Nutt.

Baked in the ashes about ten minutes (82), now obsolescent (I).

ha·šgon—*fruit of Yucca baccata* Torr.

The fruit (which P calls "wild bananas") may be cooked at any time
but must be ripe, with black seeds, in order to make the cake described
below. In late summer it is gathered, peeled by rubbing off the outer pulp
with the hands, and the seeds discarded. Bake skin and pulp over fire until
very brown, stirring constantly. When it takes on the consistency of applesauce remove to another pan and cool. Grind thoroughly on a metate until
very fine and sticky, then mold by teaspoonfuls on a flat board and dry for
five days in the sun thus forming small, red, slightly sticky cakes. Knead
these cakes into a hard dough and mold into loaves like bread, making a
lengthwise hole through each loaf, dry again for five days in the sun, and
store in boxes for the winter. Mixed with water and used for preserves with
corn breads it is something like applesauce (82). 47 said only certain women
make it, others buy from them. She learned from her mother when she
was little.

hʷoš dižo·li·—*fruit of Opuntia sp.* (F).

This fruit is eaten raw when ripe.

dižé coh—*Peaches* (F).

Dried and stored for winter, then boiled and eaten with corn foods (82).

dižé—*Prunus melanocarpa* (A. Nels.) Rydb. (F).

In the old days choke cherries were ground and eaten (82) because everything was ground; ground and made into a cake which was then dried and called ńdo·ka·dí (I) or diẓé náneska·dí (P, Q, R, S). P's husband, a well known singer, calls it diẓé łe·sʔá·ń (cherry bread) and says it is made by grinding the berries, patting them into a cake two and one-half inches in diameter, and drying it in the sun for ten days. "Any woman or young lady" (virgin?) may make it. It is used as a medicine in Mountain Top Way and Beauty Way, mixed with the mountain medicines which are given the patient, because the choke cherry is also a mountain plant.

SEASONINGS

tʔáʔáši·ʔ—*native salt.*

Deposits found in the vicinity of the Navaho reservation. It has a grayish color, is ground on a metate, and does not have the strong taste of commercial salt, therefore being preferred by some because "store salt is bitter" (82).

hazaʔale·—*Aulospermum purpureum* (Wats.) C. and R. (M).

Used to flavor corn foods since it "tastes like chili" (A, 50); used in soups, as is also *Chenopodium,* for flavoring; and after gathering in the spring dried and stored in paper bags for winter used (P, Q, R, S,). One informant refrains from using it as her children refuse food flavored thus.

táʔi·cóhi·—*squash blossoms.* (H).

Boiled with mutton tallow, salted, and eaten as a soup; added in large quantities to boiled meat for flavoring. They are often picked when very large, strung on wire, dried in the shade, and stored for winter when they are used to season meats and soups.

BEVERAGES

koh·ᵂé·ʔ—*coffee.* (F).

Arburkle's Ariosa coffee is most generally used. Not being thoroughly roasted its flavor makes one believe the pot must have previously been used for kerosene. Water is strained into the pot, one and one-half large spoons of coffee added, and boiled, with or without sugar. It is served with quantities of sugar, and canned milk.

dé·h—*tea.* (F).

Commercial tea is sometimes served, especially to guests. It is steeped on the leaves.

čil koh·ᵂé·ʔ—*Thelesperma gracile* (Torr.) Gray. "Navaho tea."

Gathered in small bundles (about six stalks each) which are folded into thirds and tied with another stalk, strung on a cord and dried. May be used either fresh or dry, one bundle being placed in a pot of cold water, brought to a boil, and boiled to the desired strength. It makes a fragrant, clear, dark-amber drink.

gad—*juniper tea.*

A hot infusion of juniper twigs, given to a woman to drink (one or two cups a day for six days) directly after childbirth "to clean out the blood" (73).

Other beverages:

Refer to seeds of Descurainia, Sporobolus, and Oryzopsis.

STORAGE OF FOODS

bį·h bici·n—*Deer meat.*

Formerly dried, cut into small pieces, and stored in buckskin sacks in a cave (A). Now obsolete since deer is not hunted (I).

Wild potatoes.

Dried whole in the sun and stored in the hogan.

našžíži—*dry shelled corn* (H).

Stored in a round hole in the ground, lined with shredded juniper bark (ʔažíʼh), covered with more bark, then a thin rock, and lastly a layer of dirt. Storage pit only known to members of the immediate family (A, 50).

Squash and Flower seeds.

Stored in the same manner as corn, in a hole three and one-half feet deep and twenty inches in diameter, only known to the family (A). Stored in a sack or pan in the hogan, and sometimes buried with other foods (F).

Roots and Seeds.

Stored in an unlined hole (previously dried out with a fire) either loose or in sacks. Removed only before dawn in order to keep the storage place a secret (50).

South Orange, N. J.

COACHWHIP PUBLICATIONS

COACHWHIPBOOKS.COM

Cherokee Cooklore

TO MAKE MY BREAD

Recipes

Herbs

Wild Foods

History

The Feast

Cherokee, North Carolina

ISBN 978-1-61646-257-4

www.ingramcontent.com/pod-product-compliance
Lightning Source LLC
Chambersburg PA
CBHW061415090426

42742CB00024B/3470